Correspondence of
Richard Hurd and William Mason

E. H. PEARCE

Bishop of Worcester 1919–1930

in the Hurd Library, Hartlebury Castle

The Correspondence of
Richard Hurd & William Mason

And Letters of Richard Hurd to
Thomas Gray

With Introduction & Notes

by the late

ERNEST HAROLD PEARCE

D.D., Litt.D., F.S.A.

Bishop of Worcester

Edited

with additional Notes by

LEONARD WHIBLEY, M.A.

Fellow of Pembroke College
Cambridge

CAMBRIDGE

AT THE UNIVERSITY PRESS

1932

CAMBRIDGE
UNIVERSITY PRESS

University Printing House, Cambridge CB2 8BS, United Kingdom

Published in the United States of America by Cambridge University Press, New York

Cambridge University Press is part of the University of Cambridge.

It furthers the University's mission by disseminating knowledge in the pursuit of
education, learning and research at the highest international levels of excellence.

www.cambridge.org
Information on this title: www.cambridge.org/9781107654785

© Cambridge University Press 1932

First published 1932
First paperback edition 2014

A catalogue record for this publication is available from the British Library

ISBN 978-1-107-65478-5 Paperback

This book, but a fragment of the life of Richard Hurd that was in contemplation, was being prepared for publication by the late Bishop of Worcester at the time of his death. It is now published at the desire, and by the help, of some of his friends.

CONTENTS

PORTRAITS

* In an unpublished letter to Christopher Alderson, dated Curzon Street, June 23rd, 1774, Mason wrote: "Stonhewer has made me sit for my picture to Sʳ Joshua Reynolds. He has taken a great deal of pains with it, and says it is the very best head he ever painted". This picture was bequeathed by Richard Stonhewer to Pembroke College, Cambridge. A replica or copy of it was painted for Henry Duncombe of Copgrove, near Knaresborough, M.P. for the County of York (born 1728, died 1818). It descended to Elizabeth, daughter of Henry John Duncombe, Rector of Kirkby Sigston, who married Henry Bramwell of Crown East, near Worcester. At a sale at Crown East in 1922, after the death of Mr Bramwell, the picture, catalogued as "Man holding a roll of paper", was bought by Rowland Alwyn Wilson, Rector of Witley, Worcester. (Information given by Canon Wilson.)

PREFACE

The late Bishop of Worcester, to whom the originals of the letters here printed were entrusted, transcribed the greater part of the text, and annotated it.

The Syndics of the Press, when they undertook the publication and requested me to act as editor, accepted the suggestion that the full text of the letters should be printed and that the notes should be revised and amplified. I have, therefore, while retaining the greater part of Bishop Pearce's notes, rewritten some of them, and have added fresh notes of my own. The best explanation or illustration of a passage in the letters is often to be found in contemporary correspondence, and other letters of Hurd and Mason, as well as letters of Warburton, Gray, Walpole, etc., have been quoted for this purpose.

The Introduction, in which the Bishop gave an account of the manuscripts and a survey of the friendship between Hurd and Mason, has been printed with the least possible change. I have added the records of events in their own lives which both Hurd and Mason left behind them.

In the bundle of the later letters which passed between Hurd and Mason there are letters written to

Hurd or to his nephew after Mason's death. Some of these are printed in an Appendix: they throw light on the circumstances, and fix the date of Mason's death: they show the interest which Hurd continued to take in what concerned Mason: he composed the epitaph to be placed on Mason's monument, and was informed of the reasons for the delay in publishing the final edition of Mason's poems. A second Appendix deals with manuscripts of poems by Gray and Mason.

My thanks are due to the Bishop of Worcester for entrusting me with the original manuscripts of the letters, so that I was enabled to complete and correct the transcription. I have also to thank the Dean of York and Mr Harrison, the Librarian of the Dean and Chapter Library, for placing at my disposal William Mason's manuscript Commonplace Book, belonging to that Library, which contains Mason's "Dates of the Principal events relative to Myself", and copies of epigrams, not hitherto recognised as by Mason, two of which are quoted in the notes.

To Canon R. A. Wilson, of Witley Rectory, Worcester, I am indebted for much friendly help, as also for the loan of nearly 140 manuscript letters, addressed by Mason to his curate Christopher Alderson. These afford valuable information and are often quoted in the notes. Canon Wilson has also allowed his portrait of Mason to be reproduced.

The Bishop of Derby and Dr Paget Toynbee read the proof-sheets and gave me the benefit of their suggestions. The Rev. W. H. Brooke, Rector of Aston, kindly gave me information concerning Mason's monument in his church. Mr H. M. Leman sent me particulars of the memorials to Gray and Mason erected by Frederick Montagu at Papplewick, which are mentioned in one of the letters.

Thanks are due to many friends for help in identifying quotations or explaining references, to Professor Edward Bensly, Professor Allardyce Nicoll, Mr A. L. Attwater, Mr R. W. Chapman, Mr H. G. Comber, Mr L. F. Powell and Professor Nicol Smith.

LEONARD WHIBLEY

January 1932

[*Notes or other matter added by the Editor are enclosed within square brackets*]

NOTE

ON THE TEXT OF THE LETTERS

In the transcription the text of the letters has been literally followed: the spelling and punctuation of the original have been kept, the same use of capitals and abbreviations followed. The letters were carefully read and docketed by Richard Hurd, the Bishop's nephew, and occasionally annotated. Initials denoting persons were filled in, or brief notes added above the line, identifying persons alluded to. Many expansions that he added have been printed, with a bracket to show the addition, in the text. Some of his identifications are obviously wrong; these have been disregarded or discussed in the notes, so far as is necessary. The letter [H] in a note indicates that it is taken from Richard Hurd's pencilled addition. It seems likely that the underlinings of words in some letters were not made by the writer to indicate emphasis, but were marks made by Richard Hurd to call his attention to particular points, and such underlinings have been ignored.

WORKS QUOTED IN THE NOTES BY ABBREVIATED TITLES

WILLIAM WARBURTON

The Works of the Right Reverend William Warburton, Lord Bishop of Gloucester. In seven volumes, 1788. [Edited by Bishop Hurd.] WORKS

A Discourse by way of General Preface to the quarto edition of Bishop Warburton's Works, containing some account of the Life, Writings, and Character of the Author. 1794. [By Bishop Hurd.] DISCOURSE

Letters from a late eminent Prelate to one of his Friends [1808]. [Edited by Bishop Hurd.] LETTERS

RICHARD HURD

The Works of Richard Hurd, D.D., Lord Bishop of Worcester. 8 vols. 1811. WORKS

Memoirs of the Life and Writings of the Right Rev. Richard Hurd, D.D. By Francis Kilvert. 1860. KILVERT

WILLIAM MASON

The Works of William Mason, M.A. 4 volumes. 1811. WORKS

The Correspondence of Horace Walpole and   WALPOLE-
the Rev. William Mason. Edited with   MASON
notes by the Rev. J. Mitford. 2 vols.   CORRE-
1851.   SPONDENCE

THOMAS GRAY

The Poems of Mr Gray to which are prefixed   POEMS
Memoirs of his Life and Writings. By   MEMOIRS
W. Mason, M.A. 1775.

The Letters of Thomas Gray. Edited by   TOVEY
Duncan C. Tovey. 3 vols. 1900–1912.

HORACE WALPOLE

The Letters of Horace Walpole. Edited by   LETTERS
Mrs Paget Toynbee. 16 vols. 1903.

INTRODUCTION

BY THE LATE DR E. H. PEARCE

It happened to me a few years ago to publish some records of the famous house which is the traditional home of the Bishops of Worcester,[1] and which I believe to be without its peer among such residences. The book contained some account of Richard Hurd, who occupied the See from 1781 to 1808. If it was to be at all complete, the book could not omit him, for he was the last to make any addition to the castle, erecting in 1782 the spacious and graceful library, which occupies the first floor of the west front, and remodelling that side of the house. At the same time, I could hardly fail to say something of the man himself, something, perhaps, which showed a certain sense of resentment against those who were apt to belittle his remarkable character and to speak slightingly of what they held to be his sycophantic attitude to Warburton. I felt certain that the little, prim, precise Bishop was a much more considerable personage than these critics realised.

Soon after the issue of the book some friends in Worcester, who through previous generations of their family had had professional connexion with the Bishop and with some survivors of his family, informed me that they were in possession of a collection of papers and relics which, they believed, had for many years ceased to have any legal owner. They could see that

[1] [*Hartlebury Castle*. By Ernest Harold Pearce, London, 1926.]

I was personally interested in the man himself. More-over, I was for the moment the occupant of the great office in the Church which he held for nearly thirty years, and which not even Lambeth could tempt him to lay down. I was also living in and, as far as I could, caring for the house which he at great cost had adorned. Was it not natural, they suggested, that these Hurd archives should be deposited at Hartlebury Castle?

I, of course, was more than delighted to consent. My car transported the precious relics to their old home. They fill a bureau, on the landing of the main staircase just outside his library door—a bureau which is part of the furniture that he so well knew how to choose in an age when fine furniture was to be had for the choosing. So they have become part of the property of the See, till some claimant arises who may prove an inherited right to take them away.

There followed, of course, some delightful moments, not many continuously, in which I could examine these treasures and discover their contents. I soon found everywhere the traces of the docketing and in-vestigating care of the Bishop's nephew—also named Richard Hurd, and familiarly Dickie—the inseparable companion and support of his uncle's declining years.[2] There are some pathetic genealogical efforts to probe

[2] [Richard Hurd, the son of Hurd's brother Thomas, went to live at Hartlebury Castle soon after his uncle became Bishop of Worcester. In 1783 he was appointed Registrar of the diocese, and had his office at the Palace in Worcester. He was his uncle's companion and secretary, he catalogued the books in the library and annotated the documents. After Hurd's death he lived in the Palace at Worcester and continued to act as Registrar until his death in 1827.]

into the past of this family of simple Staffordshire yeomen. There are papers dealing with the governance of Brewood School, whence Hurd passed on to Emmanuel College, which is also represented in the collection. There is much correspondence with Charles Yorke, the ill-fated Lord Chancellor of a few hours, with regard to Hurd's appointment by the Benchers of Lincoln's Inn to the preachership of their chapel in succession to Warburton. There are many papers and letters connected with the Bishop's work as tutor to the two eldest sons of George III. All his chief ecclesiastical credentials are in evidence—his benefices, his archdeaconry, his two Sees, first Coventry and Lichfield, and then Worcester, with his bonds for First-Fruits and the "tips" he paid at St James's when he did homage. There is also a considerable body of miscellaneous correspondence, carefully listed in the neat script of Dickie; and there are some pitiful data for chronicling the Bishop's last days; indeed, the very passages of Holy Scripture which the nephew read to him as he lay dying are all recorded. Long biographies have been constructed out of much less material. I should much like to put it all within reasonable compass, if life and opportunity are granted to me.

Among these treasures were Hurd's letters to and from William Mason, Precentor of York and Rector of Aston, the typical parson-poet of the eighteenth century, Warburton's friend and Gray's biographer. Mason's friendship and correspondence with Gray are fully known. His letters to and from Walpole have long been accessible in print. These Mason-Hurd letters, the approved survivors of a winnowing which the Hurds themselves applied to a larger collection after Mason's death, ought to be equally accessible.

A few months after Mason's death the Rev. Christopher Alderson, the executor of Mason's will, sent to the Bishop one hundred and thirty of Hurd's letters, which the poet had kept. With the bundle there is a careful note in Richard's handwriting that the first collection, forty-five in number, extended from 7 May 1747 to the end of 1759; the second, also forty-five, from 1760 to the end of 1769; and the third, forty in number, from 1770 to the end of 1790. There follows the statement that they were "returned to Bishop Hurd after the death of Mr Mason, by the Reverend Charles Alderson,[3] his sole Executor, 5 January 1798". Richard Hurd added to his note: "in 1821 destroyed 100 of the above Letters, 30 remaining, 7 May 1747 to 18 Oct. 1773". Besides these thirty letters,[4] which belong to the earlier correspondence, there is a second bundle of letters, twenty-three in number, written between 1788 and 1797, four being from Hurd to Mason and nineteen from Mason to Hurd.[5]

From these two bundles we may reconstruct the long friendship between Richard Hurd and William Mason. Hurd, as he often says, was a man of few friends. He

[3] Charles is a mistake for Christopher. The Rev. Christopher Alderson was for many years Mason's curate at Aston, in which capacity Gray described him as "a good creature" (Tovey, III, p. 159). At the time of Mason's death he was Rector of Eckington, Derbyshire, and he followed Mason as incumbent of Aston.

[4] Letters I–XI, XVI–XXV, XXVII–XXXV. Letter XXXVI is not in either bundle. See p. 94, n. 1.

[5] Letters XXXVII–LIX. There is also a packet of letters from Hurd to Thomas Gray (inscribed "My Letters to Mr Gray returned to me after his death by Mr Mason"). The letters are printed below: Letters XII–XV, XXVI. Other papers connected with Gray are printed in Appendix B.

never wore his heart upon his sleeve. He could never have compassed that facile bonhomie which constitutes the popularity of modern bishops. But his friendship with Mason was one of the fundamental interests of his life. Its only equals were his admiration for Warburton and his affection for Balguy. The former of these can be realised from his biographical Discourse prefixed to his edition of Warburton's *Works*; the latter is known to readers of Kilvert's life of Hurd. But before he had crossed Warburton's path Hurd learnt to know Mason. Hurd's friendship with Mason, like his friendship with Warburton, began in a critic's sympathy, and he never ceased to watch with firm but friendly and almost paternal criticism over all that Mason wrote. From the first Hurd's judgment appreciated Mason's literary efforts; his insight saw that better things were still to come; his personal attachment was the consequence.

Criticism, of course, was Hurd's accepted *métier*, whether he was dealing with Warburton or Balguy or Mason. Those who deride his relation to Warburton as mere toadyism mistake the man. Warburton was the oldest of the group, and a man whose position was assured before the others came to any note; and for this reason Hurd's criticisms of him and advice to him had their note of deference and respect. But it was criticism all the same, the comment of a man who never hesitated to speak his mind, and who hesitated all the less because in his somewhat frigid way he entertained a real affection for the person to whom the criticism might be addressed.

It is only to this extent that his attitude to Mason

differs from his attitude to Warburton. When he and Mason were still in their youth, with their future unknown, he would warn his friend against "having anything to do with great lords in the North": "all that you and I want to learn is to be content with a little, and then we can be happier than great men, falsely so called, can make us".[6] When the "seventies" had come upon both of them, and Hurd had long been in high station, while Mason was still Precentor of York Minster, the friendship subsists on the old conditions. Mason will submit all his work, and the Bishop will say about it what seems to him good. The poet, for instance, wrote a septuagenarian sonnet. The last two lines, the critic suggested, "might be expressed more happily"; and so they were. But along with the criticism went " fervent wishes that you may live to write many more birthday Sonnets".[7] Or the poet writes an epitaph for some worthy Yorkshire lady, and Mason is found writing to Hurd in gratitude for his "strictures"[8] upon it. Again Hurd disliked the last line and a half; but now the poet was "obliged to be restive".[9] After all, the lines had only said that the good lady, a great sufferer, added Hope to Faith and Charity. There was no doubt she had done so, said Mason; I knew her and you did not; why should I not say it?

Thus, if the critic is inclined to be magisterial, it is only on the lines of a long and intimate friendship which expects to be trusted all the time about everything. "Why may I not be permitted to see your Argentile?" asks Hurd.[10] When after Gray's death

[6] L. IV.   [7] L. XLIV.   [8] L. XLVIII, n. 8.
[9] L. XLVIII, n. 9.   [10] L. XXVIII.

Mason had the disposal of all his papers, Hurd was the first of his friends from whom he sought advice.[11] The gossip who considered that there was "an interregnum in the friendship" between Hurd and Mason, because he was convinced that Hurd had never been consulted about Gray's *Memoirs*, was wrong.[12] When the book was in preparation, "I shall be glad to see the sheets", writes Hurd, "as they come out of the Prefs".[13] And the letters show that Mason submitted parts of them to Hurd and received his criticisms.[14]

Presently it was the turn of the criticised. Hurd had long been concerned to put forward what he believed to be the true view of Warburton, and prepared the famous Discourse with infinite care. It was critical where criticism seemed justifiable, but the greatness of the man must not be belittled to satisfy the rancour of his enemies. Nevertheless, might it not be better that Hurd and Warburton should both be in their graves before the Discourse was published? The question was put by the Bishop to Mason, not in a letter, but face to face, when the poet was paying one of his periodical visits to Hartlebury, and the poet was all for publishing at once. "What you said to me", the Bishop wrote in

[11] [In an unpublished letter of Mason to Christopher Alderson of 8 Dec. 1771, he writes: "I shall go to Town, that I may have a better opportunity of consulting D͏͆ Hurd both about M͏͆ Gray's poetical matters and my own".]
[12] [The reference is to Joseph Cradock, who, in his *Literary and Miscellaneous Memoirs*, I, p. 182, wrote: "It was about this period that Mason's Life of Gray was advertised....I then perceived that there was an interregnum in the friendship between him and Mason, for as soon as I looked over the book I was fully convinced that *he* had never been consulted about the publication".]
[13] L. XXXIII.   [14] LL. XXXIV, XXXV.

his next letter, "had it's proper weight...I have sent the Bp.'s Life to the press".[15]

The friendship between Hurd and Mason must have begun in Mason's undergraduate days. Mason was admitted pensioner at St John's College on 1 July 1742, and went into residence in the following October. His first tutor, Mr Wrigley, was presented to a College living in 1743, and his departure placed Mason under the sympathetic tutelage of William Samuel Powell, for which the young man was properly grateful. Powell had returned to St John's in 1742 as assistant tutor and became principal tutor in 1744, and within two years Mason gave expression of his obligations in his *Ode on leaving St John's College, Cambridge*.[16]

"There still", he wrote in his farewell to Cambridge,

> There still shall Gratitude her tribute pay
> To him who first approv'd my infant lay;
> And fair to Recollection's eyes
> Shall POWELL's various virtues rise.

It was, no doubt, to Powell that Mason owed his introduction to Hurd,[17] a close friend of Powell[18] and

---

[15] L. XL.

[16] Mason, *Works*, I, p. 27. The Ode is dated 1746.

[17] [Hurd was five years Mason's senior; he had entered Emmanuel College in 1735, and had taken his Master's degree in 1742, before Mason matriculated. He was ordained in the same year and for a time was in charge of Reymerston, a Norfolk parish, but, after his election to a fellowship at Emmanuel, he returned into residence early in 1743.]

[18] Powell and Hurd both graduated in 1738–9; both received priest's orders from Dr Gooch, Bishop of Norwich; Powell going (at least nominally) to a Norfolk benefice in the gift of Lord Townshend, to whose son he was tutor, and Hurd to the curacy of Reymerston in the same county. Another intimate friend of both Powell and Hurd was Thomas Balguy, assistant tutor of St John's, whose acquaintance with Mason grew into friendship.

of Balguy, who was then assistant tutor at St John's. The friendship of Hurd and Mason must have ripened rapidly, for within a year of Mason's leaving Cambridge, Hurd was writing to Mason in terms that imply an easy intimacy.

How close and constant was their friendship is shown by the letters that passed between them for fifty years.[19] And when the news of Mason's death at Aston, on 5 April 1797, reached Hartlebury, the old Bishop took out his commonplace book[20] and gave characteristic expression to his feelings and his memories:

Mason (Rev. William)—Residentiary & Precentor of York, and Rector of Aston near Rotheram, died Apr. 5. 1797. I had known him from a youth at St John's College, Cambridge, where he was educated under my worthy friend, Mr Powell. Our friendship continued thro' life. With many other virtues, he poſseſsed a fine genius for poetry, and was indeed the best poet of his time, as appears from his works of that sort published by himself, at different times, in *three* volumes.[21] He also wrote the lives of *his* two ingenious friends, and mine, Mr Gray and Mr Whitehead. The last production of his pen was an Ode, formed upon the 28th chapter of the book of Job, of wch he printed a few copies. One of these he sent to me a few days before his death, with a friendly dedication to me prefixed. It is called in the title page, *a private copy*: for he intended not to publish it, at least at that time,

[19] [There was for a time an interruption of the friendship and the correspondence. See below, pp. 95 ff.]
[20] Vol. II, p. 368.
[21] The following are the Hartlebury Library copies: *Poems*, by William Mason, M.A., 1764, inscribed "The Author's present to R. Hurd"; new edition, 1771; fifth edition, 1779; *Poems*, by William Mason, M.A., vol. III, "now first published", 1797; *The English Garden*, new edition corrected, 1783; and *Works* of William Mason, M.A., in four volumes, 1811, which must have been purchased by Richard Hurd, junior, and which he interleaved after his careful fashion.

but to present it to some select friends. He had entered into his 72$^{\underline{d}}$ year on 23$^{\underline{rd}}$ of February last: yet this lyrical composition is not inferiour in merit to any others he had ever produced. With a tast for all the polite arts, and with no small proficiency in them. He was an excellent parish priest, and will be long remembered with respect and veneration at Aston where he usually resided, and where he dyed. He took much delight in that place, and built an excellent house upon it. The Garden about it was not large; but laid out with that tast, wch was to be expected from the author of *The English Garden.* Vale, amicifsime!

R. W. 1797.

[RECORDS

OF THE PRINCIPAL EVENTS OF THE LIVES OF *RICHARD HURD* AND *WILLIAM MASON* WRITTEN BY THEMSELVES]

The following tables were drawn up by Hurd and Mason themselves. Hurd's list,[1] written in his own hand and endorsed by him "Some occurrences in my Life. R.W.", was found amongst his papers after his death: it had been continued almost to the last, and the concluding paragraph was written only five weeks before he died.

Mason's list,[2] headed "Memorandums or Dates of the Principal events relative to Myself", was written in his *Commonplace Book*. After 1773 he made no further entries.

I

HURD'S LIST OF EVENTS

Dates of some Occurrences in my own Life

A.D.

Richard Hurd was born at Congreve, in the Parish of Penkrick, in the County of Stafford, January   1719–20

---

[1] Printed in the *Works of Richard Hurd, D.D.* (1811), I, pp. vii ff. Details not relevant to the correspondence with Mason have been omitted, including all entries after the date of Mason's death.

[2] The *Commonplace Book* is in the Dean and Chapter Library at York. Mitford published Mason's list with many serious mistakes. (*Walpole-Mason Correspondence*, II, pp. 411–12.)

He was the second of three children, all sons of John and Hannah Hurd; plain, honest and good people.

There being a good Grammar School at Brewood, he was educated there under the Reverend Mᴿ Hillman, and upon his death, under his succefsor, the Reverend Mᴿ Budworth—both well qualified for their office and both very kind to him.

Under so good direction, he was thought fit for the University, and was accordingly admitted in Emanuel College, in Cambridge, October 3,   1733 but did not go to reside there till a year or two afterwards.

In this college, he was happy in receiving the countenance, and in being permitted to attend the Lectures, of that excellent Tutor, Mᴿ Henry Hubbard, although he had been admitted under another person.

He took his B.A.'s degree in   1738–9

He took his M.A.'s degree, and was elected fellow in   1742

Was ordained Deacon, 13ᵗʰ of June that year.

Was ordained Priest, 20 May   1744

He took his B.D.'s degree in   1749

He published the same year Remarks on Mᴿ Werton's book on the *Rejection of Heathen Miracles*, and his Commentary on Horace's *Ars Poetica*; which last book introduced him to the acquaintance of Mᴿ Warburton, by whose recommendation to the Bishop of London, Dᴿ Sherlock, he was appointed Whitehall Preacher in May   1750

He published the Commentary on the Epistle to Augustus in   1751

—the new edition of both Comments, with Dedication to Mᴿ Warburton in   1753

—the Difsertation on the Delicacy of Friendship in   1755

His Father died Nov. 27 this year, æt. 70.

xxvi

He published the Remarks on Hume's Natural History of Religion in — 1757

Was instituted this year, Feb. 16, to the Rectory of Thurcaston, in the County of Leicester, on the presentation of Emanuel College.

He published Moral and Political Dialogues — 1759

He had the Sine-cure Rectory of Folkton near Bridlington, Yorkshire, given him by the Lord Chancellor on the recommendation of M.ʳ Allen, of Prior Park, near Bath, November 2, — 1762

He published the Letters on Chivalry and Romance this year.

—Dialogues on Foreign Travel in — 1763

And Letter to D.ʳ Leland of Dublin in — 1764

He was made Preacher of Lincoln's Inn, on the recommendation of M.ʳ Charles Yorke, &c., November 6, — 1765

Was collated to the Archdeaconry of Gloucester by the Bishop, August 27, — 1767

Was appointed to open the Lecture of Bishop Warburton on Prophecy in — 1768

He took the Degree of D.D. at Cambridge Commencement this year.

He published the Sermons on Prophecy in — 1772

His Mother died Feb. 27, 1773, æt. 88 — 1773

He was consecrated Bishop of Lichfield and Coventry, the 12.ᵗʰ of February — 1775

He published the 1st Volume of Sermons preached at Lincoln's Inn — 1776

And was made Preceptor to the Prince of Wales and his brother Prince Frederick the 5.ᵗʰ of June the same year.

He lost his old and best friend, Bishop Warburton, June 7.ᵗʰ — 1779

He published the 2d and 3d Volumes of Sermons in — 1780

The Bishop of Winchester [D.ʳ Thomas] died Tuesday, May 1, 1781. Received a gracious letter from his Majesty next day with the offer of — 1781

xxvii

the see of Worcester, in the room of Bishop North, to be translated to Winchester, and of the Clerkship of the Closet, in the room of the late Bishop of Winchester.

On his arrival at Hartlebury Castle in July that year, resolved to put the Castle into complete order, and to build a Library, which was much wanted.

The Library was finished in   1782 and furnished with a collection of books, late Bishop Warburton's, and ordered by his will to be sold   1783

To these, other considerable additions have been since made.

Archbishop Cornwallis died in 1783.

Had the offer of the Archbishoprick from his Majesty, with many gracious expressions, and pressed to accept it; but humbly begged leave to decline it, as a charge not suited to his temper and talents, and much too heavy for him to sustain, especially in these times.

Put the last hand (at least he thinks so) to the Bishop of Gloucester's Life, to be prefixed to the new edition of his works now in the prefs   1785

In the end of February this year   1788 was published in seven volumes 4to a complete edition of the works of Bishop Warburton. The *Life* is omitted for the present.

This summer the King came to Cheltenham to drink the waters, and was attended by the Queen, the Princess Royal, and the Princesses Augusta and Elizabeth. On Saturday, August the second, They were pleased to visit Hartlebury. The Duke of York came from London to Cheltenham the day before, and was pleased to come with them. They arrived at Hartlebury at half an hour past eleven. ...About two o'clock, their Majesties, &c., returned to Cheltenham.

On the Tuesday following, August the fifth, their Majesties with the three Princesses, arrived at 8 o'clock in the evening at the Bishop's Palace in Worcester, to attend the charitable meeting of the three Quires of Worcester, Hereford and Gloucester....

On Saturday morning, Aug. 9th, the King and Queen, &c., returned to Cheltenham.

My younger Brother, M.ʳ Thomas Hurd of Birmingham, died on Saturday, Sept. 17,   1791

My elder Brother, Mr John Hurd, of Hatton, near Shifnal, died on Thursday, December 6,   1792

My noble and honoured friend, the Earl of Mansfield, died March 20,   1793

My old and much esteemed friend, D.ʳ Balguy, Prebendary and Archdeacon of Winchester, died January 19,   1795

The Life of Bishop Warburton, which was sent to the prefs in Autumn last, was not printed off till the end of January, nor published till the end of February this year.

Printed in the course of this year at the Kidderminster prefs a Collection of Bishop Warburton's Letters to me, to be published after my death for the benefit of the Worcester Infirmary. The edition consisted of 250 Copies, 4to—was finished at the prefs in the beginning of December.

In the Summer of 1796 visited my Diocese in Person, I have great reason to suppose for the last time; being in the 77ᵗʰ year of my age—*fiat voluntas Dei!*   1796 June 17–30

M.ʳ Mason died at Aston, April 5,   1797

He was one of my oldest and most respected friends. How few of this description now remain!

II

MASON'S LIST OF EVENTS

*Memorandums or Dates of the Principal events
relative to Myself*

Born Feb. 12th 1724 Old Style.
My Mother died in childbed the Christmas following.
Admitted Pensioner at St Johns College Cambridge under
Mr Wrigley June 30th 1743.[1] Elected Schollar of that
College the October following.
Nominated by the fellows of Pembroke to a fellowship in that
Society, (a Dispute having arisen between them and the
Master concerning the right of Election) when middle
Batchelor 1747.
This dispute being compromisd was admitted a Fellow by
the Master in Feb. 1749.[2]
Admitted to the degree of Master of Arts July 1749.
Went into Orders, was instituted to the Living of Aston and
appointed Chaplain to the Earl of Holdernefse in November
1754.
My Father died Augst 26th 1753.
Arch Bishop Hutton gave me the Prebend of Holme in the
Church of York Dec. 6th 1756.
Appointed by the Duke of Devonshire Chaplain in Ordinary
to K. George the 2^d Augst 1757.
Resigned a Bye Fellowship of Pembroke (wch was given me
by that Society after my Foundation Fellowship became
vacant on institution to Aston[3]) 1759.
Appointed Chaplain to his Present Majesty Sep^t 19, 1761.
Dr Fountayne Dean of York made me Canon residentiary of
that Cathedral. Jan. 7th 1762.

[1] The date should be 1 July 1742.
[2] He was elected Fellow on March 2 and admitted on March 16.
[3] He had a year of grace after his institution and vacated his
Fellowship in December 1755. See L. VIII, n. 9. On March 23,
1756, he was elected to a Bye Fellowship on Mr Smart's Foundation.

Installd Precentor of the same Church on the Resignation of D.ʳ Newton Bishop of Bristol, and on that acc.ᵗ in his Majestys Gift. Feb. 22.ᵈ 1762.

Resigned the same day to ArchBishop Drummond the Prebend of Holme, on receiving the Prebend of Driffield annext to the Precentorship.

Married Mary the daughter of W. Sherman Esqr of Hull. Sep.ᵗ 25.ᵗʰ 1765.

She died of a consumption at Bristol March 27.ᵗʰ 1767.

Ah amantiſsima Optima fœmina Vale!

John Hutton Esqr.ᵉ of Marske near Richmond Yorkshire died Jan.ʳʸ 12.ᵗʰ 1768 by whose death an Estate in the East riding came to me in reversion.

M.ʳ Gray died July 30.ᵗʰ 1771 & left me his executor jointly with D.ʳ Brown Master of Pembroke Hall.

Resignd my Chaplainship to the King Aug: 1773.[4]

[4] Mason wrote Sonnet III (*Works*, I, p. 123) apparently to celebrate his release from the duties of his chaplaincy. This he dated "August, 1773". In spite of this and of the definite statement above, there is no doubt that he resigned his chaplaincy before the end of 1772.

RICHARD HURD
Bishop of Worcester 1781–1808

I

HURD *to* Mason

Dear Sir

I am just return'd from a fortnight's ramble into Norfolk;[1] wch must be my Excuse for not acknowledging, so soon as I ought, your present of Musæus.[2] This Piece has now had it's fate; & tho' you must have known it long since from other hands, I must have leave to say that ev'ry body here reads & admires it, nothing ever pleas'd so generally. It has caught all sorts of Readers from Heads of Colleges down to little Coffee-House Critics. If there be here & there a little Envy, it dares not so much as shew itself in faint praises. Ev'ry one is asham'd not to appear struck, with what charms ev'ry body. Don't suspect me of flattery: I am only making a true & faithful Report, which I do with the greater pleasure as I hope this early tast of honest fame, a motive which a Poet may freely avow & the noblest indeed that can excite to any Undertaking, will engage you without further scruple to complete your other Imitations of Milton.[3] The succefs of anything you do hereafter is certain; ev'n if one may suppose it to have much lefs merit than Musæus, which nothing I am sure of your's can ever

---

[1] On his ordination in 1742 (E. H. Pearce, *Hartlebury Castle*, p. 279) Hurd accepted a curacy at Reymerston, near Attleborough. His local friendships with Cox Macro, the antiquary, Robert Nash, Chancellor of Norwich diocese, and others, can be gathered from Kilvert, *Hurd*, pp. 10–15. At Reymerston he read *Pamela*.

[2] *Musæus: A Monody to the Memory of Mr Pope*, by Mr Mason, was published by Dodsley on 17 April 1747. It was written in 1744.

[3] [*Il Bellicoso* and *Il Pacifico* were written in 1744 some time before *Musæus*. See Mason, *Works*, 1, p. 158.]

I

have.[4] I know you are in pain, till I quit this Subject; but you must allow me to say, it gives me the greatest Joy to observe this public testimony to the merit of a Person, who has hitherto been so unjust to Himself, as by all means to conceal it. And I could not resist the pleasure of persecuting you with some part of the Applause, you fly from, ev'n tho' I follow'd you to that very Hawthorn-shade,[5] which, you hop'd, might secure you from it.

Next to Musæus, the Thing, that occasions most noise here is a piece of D.ʳ Middleton's,[6] which undertakes to overthrow the Credit of the Fathers. You may not perhaps be much interested in Theological Disputes; but as a Composition only, it may chance to entertain you. A Postscript very well exposes an absurd whimsy of D.ʳ Chapman.[7] Since this Attack upon the

---

[4] Nearly half a century later Hurd was still of the same opinion. In his *Discourse* on the life of Warburton (1794), pp. 41 f., he referred to Pope's death as having "brought on the dawn of M.ʳ Mason's genius", and added that *Musæus* "gave so sure a presage of his future eminence in poetry, and so advantageous a picture of his mind, that M.ʳ Warburton, on the sight of it

'With open arms received one poet more'"

[Pope, *Prologue to the Satires*, l. 142]. It must be acknowledged that Mason was still alive when this was printed; indeed, it was shown to him before it was printed.

[5] Mason, *Works* (1811), I, p. 15, the last canto of *Musæus*: "Unseen, unheard, beneath an hawthorn shade".

[6] In the same month in which *Musæus* was published appeared Conyers Middleton's *Introductory Discourse to a larger Work, designed hereafter to be published, concerning the miraculous Powers, which are supposed to have subsisted in the Christian Church from the earliest Ages, through several successive Centuries.* Its intention was "to fix the religion of Protestantism on its proper basis, that is, on the sacred Scriptures; not on the authority of weak & fallible man" (p. lxxvi).

[7] Middleton included "a Postscript, containing some Remarks on an Archidiaconal Charge, delivered last Summer by the Revd.

antient Fathers, another with equal Violence has been made upon a certain modern one. And to heighten the surprize Dux fœmina facti—that is to say, the old Lady of Yorkshire has fallen tooth & nail upon Dᵣ Rutherforth, set on too by Mᵣ Warburton,[8] who leads her to the Ring, & in a short Speech, after the old Homerical mode of Taunt & Defiance, commits Her to the Engagement. The Short of the story is, that the old Lady writes with a Spirit below her Years tho' 'tis observ'd of Her, that She has reason in Her rage & upon the whole seems to have pretty well expos'd that very foolish Book, call'd an Efsay upon Virtue.[9] This is all the literary News I know of worth sending. In return you must tell me what grove has shelter'd you & the Muse, & what new Designs She has put upon you in your Retirement. Genial Suns and blue Skies are strong Incitements; above all in this fav'rite month, wᶜʰ no Son of the Muse ever let pafs without some poetical tribute to it. Sᵣ Edwᵈ

Dᵣ Chapman" (on 'Popery the true bane of Letters'). John Chapman was the Tory candidate for the Provostship of King's at the contested election after Snape's death (A. Austen Leigh, *King's College*, p. 196). His "whimsy" was concerned with "certain Loyolites in France", who were determined "by one desperate, furious push, to stab the Protestant cause to the heart" (Middleton, *op. cit.* p. lxxix). Middleton's phrases for it were "solemn trifles" and "elaborate nonsense"; he urged that such a treatment of the matter "adds a real force and sting to the railleries of the Sceptics" (pp. lxxxv, xcv).

[8] [Hurd did not make Warburton's acquaintance until he published Horace's *Ars Poetica* in 1749.]

[9] Catharine Cockburn, wife of Patrick Cockburn, drew up in 1747 an answer to the *Essay on the Nature and Obligations of Vertue*, 1744, by Thomas Rutherforth, D.D., F.R.S., Archdeacon of Essex and (from 1756) Regius Professor of Divinity at Cambridge. The matter is referred to in Hurd's *Discourse* on the life of Warburton (1794), p. 42, and Warburton's clever letter to the lady is printed there as Appendix B, p. 147; 26 Jan. 1745.

Littleton[10] (who is just come in from his Journey out of Staffordshire & sends Services & thanks for your Poem) prevents my saying anything more at present but that I am always, with an entire respect,

Dear Sir,

Your most Faithfull Friend and Servant,

Camb.   R. HURD

7 May 1747[11]

II

HURD *to* Mason

Dear Sir,

I expect with great pleasure your Epistle on Fashion[1], wch will be sure to find me in College & am glad to hear, y^t, notwithstanding the Muse has been bed-rid, She has been able to produce thus much. Tho' you Poets are perhaps not the more lazy for appearing to be so. Your trade may go on, seu *lectulus* aut vos porticus excepit.[2]

[10] Edward Littleton, fourth baronet (succeeded 1742), belonged to Hurd's Staffordshire interests and lived at Teddesley. He had been a pupil of Hurd's master, William Budworth, at Brewood School. He entered at Emmanuel College as a nobleman in 1744, became Hurd's pupil and was by him introduced to the circle. In 1757 Hurd dedicated to Sir Edward his edition of the *Ars Poetica*. "I had the honour", he says, "to be intrusted with a part of your education, and it was my duty to contribute all I could to the success of it. But the task was easy and pleasant". Hurd, *Works* (1811), I, p. 10. Littleton was M.P. for Staffordshire from 1784 to 1807.

[11] This and the two following letters are addressed to "Mr Mason at the Revd Mr Mason's in Hull, Yorkshire".

[1] *The Birth of Fashion*, described as "An Epistolary Tale. Written in the year 1746, and sent to a Lady with Hollar's Habits of English Women, published in the former Century 1650". Mason, *Works*, I, p. 149.

[2] Horace, *Satires*, I, iv, 134.

4

You are very Kind in not forgetting Pope's Head,[3] which I want very much to preside over the little band of worthies, which I am collecting for the ornament of my Study. If you would but, at some leisure time, contrive to give me a Sketch of your own from Hayman's[4] picture, it would complete the Obligation.

This Afternoon I have seen a small Poem of Mr Nevile's[5] (for the fame of Musæus has kindled up a flame which I thought expiring) call'd an Eſsay in the Art of writing Tragedy. The Eſsay-way, you know, has been worn quite thread-bare. But there are some fine paſsages in it, &, with a little Alteration, would be worth your seeing.

As you promise to be a better Correspondent for the future, & here are no Compliments, I shall depend on the favour of a Letter very soon. The Swaggerer and Sr Edward send Services & I am,

Dear Sir,
Your most Affectionate Friend &
Hble Servt

Camb.   R. HURD

30 May 1747

[3] See L. III, n. 1.

[4] [Hurd alludes to the vignette on the title-page of Mason's *Musæus*. This represented Chaucer, Spenser and Milton with Pope, after a design by Francis Hayman.]

[5] [Thomas Nevile, a friend of Hurd, Mason and Gray, matriculated from Jesus College in 1738; he migrated to Emmanuel in January 1745–6, and while there took his B.A. degree. He was elected a Fellow of Jesus in 1746. In 1758 he published, under his own name, *Imitations of Horace*, but he had previously issued imitations of single satires or epistles (see L. VII, n. 3). In 1767 his *Translation of the Georgics of Virgil* appeared, and in 1769 *Imitations of Juvenal and Persius*. William Cole, in a note written in 1776, described him as "of a good gentleman's family in Lincolnshire, tall and thin; he has an impediment in his speech, which may occasion much solitariness and is a layman".]

III

HURD *to* Mason

[*Cambridge, June or July 1747*][1]

Dear Sir

I am much oblig'd by your favour of Pope's head[2], which I received safe, & shall value, as it deserves, extremely. Your letter, instead of bringing the long-expected poem on Drefs, puts me off with an Excuse, which has so much ceremony in it that, for friendship's sake, I could wish you had not made it. You bid me neither "scold nor repeat the Request", which, it must be own'd, are two very reasonable Injunctions, considering that you ought certainly to expect both. However I shall so far conform to them, as to leave it

---

[1] Contrary to Hurd's custom the letter is not dated. His nephew has endorsed it "1747, about Mʳ Warburton's Shakespeare &c.". The reference to the elections, which began on June 26 of that year and were finished in July, shows that it was written towards the end of June or early in the next month. This is confirmed by the fact that Hurd had recently seen Gray's *Ode on a Distant Prospect of Eton College*, and Warburton's *Shakespeare*, both of which were published in May 1747.

[2] The reference is to a sketch of Pope's head which Hurd must have transferred from his study at Emmanuel to his study at Thurcaston, and thence later to Eccleshall and to Hartlebury, where his successors have had charge of it to this day. It hangs in his library in a group near the bust of Lord Mansfield. Mrs Pope, the poet's mother, is there, and there is an engraving of Pope after Kneller, as well as one of the monument which Warburton's officious zeal erected in Twickenham Church, as if Pope's "et sibi" tablet to his parents were not enough. Nor is there any question that the "Pope's Head" is the one with which we are concerned; for it is thus inscribed underneath:

ΟΥΤΟΣ ΕΚΕΙΝΟΣ   MVSAEVS

Mʳ Pope.

E Descriptione J. Richardson.   W. Mason Delineavit.

The artist and the occasion are thus put beyond doubt.

6

to your own conscience, whether "a want of finishing" should be a pretence for denying me so much pleasure, as everything of your's gives me.

Your new Canon of Criticism[3] is very ingenious, &, to say the truth, shrewdly urg'd against the Authenticity of the Ode on Eaton.[4] Yet 'tis confidently giv'n out here to be M.ʳ Grey's, & perhaps it may save the honour of your new-invented rule, if we suppose it printed, with the consent indeed of M.ʳ G., but not under his direction. And this, it seems, was the case; for it was the force of friendly importunity, we are told, that drew it from him. And, to shew how little He interested Himself in it's fame, He ev'n suffer'd it to paſs with ill-plac'd Capitals & wooden Ornaments. I remember to have just seen it at the Coffee-House, &, if I might presume to criticise so delicate an Author, should pronounce it to be a common thought, indifferently executed. This is dogmatically said, but I am just come from the reading of the new Edition of Shakespeare by M.ʳ Warburton,[5] a Gentleman, you know, in whose company one does not usually pick up much civility. But what He wants in Compliment, He makes up in Sense & Ingenuity, two things, which, as

[3] [Mason must have suggested that the Eton Ode was not by Gray. It is not clear what his "Canon of Criticism" was.]

[4] The *Ode on a Distant Prospect of Eton College*, "the first English production of M.ʳ Gray which appeared in print", as Mason described it, appeared anonymously on 30 May 1747. [By this time Mason had made the acquaintance of Gray, who was living as a fellow-commoner in Peterhouse. We do not know when Hurd's acquaintance began. See L. XII, n. 1.]

[5] Warburton's edition of Shakespeare was also published in May 1747, and the eight volumes which Hurd bought are still in the Hartlebury library. Hurd was at present studying Warburton's personality at a distance. They began to correspond two years later.

they are very rare, cannot fail of pleasing, in a Critic. My main quarrel against Him is for his Abuse of our friend D.ʳ Grey,[6] whom, tho' his notes on Hudibras may deserve all, that can be said of them, yet, for his own good nature, one would wish not to see so publicly insulted.

Sir Edward & I stay here much longer, than we intended, w.ᶜʰ is chiefly owing to the noise & fury of Elections. It is, I think, time enough for a young Gentleman to be initiated in the Mysteries of Party, which serves to no other end, that I know of, than to corrupt the heart & byaſs the Understanding. This conduct will, I know, be censur'd by some; but, for my own part, I had rather see any one, I am concern'd with, a candid, rational man, than the staunchest Wig, or honestest Tory in England. Sir Ed:'s compliments attend you, and I am,

Dear Sir

Your most oblig'd & Faithfull

Hble Serv.ᵗ

R. HURD

M.ʳ Powell[7] is not in College.

---

[6] Zachary Grey, LL.D., Trinity Hall, whose "Hudibras... corrected" appeared in 1744. Warburton, in his *Shakespeare*, 1, pp. xxvi f., remarks in his preface upon the recent progress of the textual criticism of the great English poets and starts aside to attack Grey: "If the follies of particular men were sufficient to bring any Branch of Learning into disrepute, I don't know any that would stand in a worse situation than that for which I now apologize. For I hardly think there ever appeared, in any *learned* language, so execrable a heap of nonsense, under the name of Commentaries, as hath been lately given on a certain satiric Poet, of the last Age, by his Editor and Coadjutor". The attack was the cause of a wordy controversy.
[7] See *Introduction*, p. xxii.

IV

HURD *to* Mason

Dear Mr Mason

I am thus far on my way to Norfolk,¹ for wch I set out to-morrow, with hopes of coming to you² on Saturday next or very soon after.

You expect to be congratulated on the succefs of your Orator.³ Tho' I question if the disappointment, tho' it may chagrin for the present, will do the other⁴ any real hurt. On the contrary, I, who hold that all things work together for good, I mean for the advancement of such as diligently seek and perfectly deserve preferment, am of opinion that it may do him much present credit and recommend him to some future service. At least I seemed to collect this much this morning from a conversation with one who usually speaks the sense of the great world and was, I found, well informed in the circumstances of the case and the reasons of R[ofs]'s disappointment. But of this not a word, for I come from the schools of wise men, of whom I have learnt the golden rule of caution. To you perhaps I may hereafter explain myself more particularly. But for the present I say no more, and ev'n for this little exact silence.

---

¹ Not his first visit to the county that year, for he had preached the Assize Sermon in Norwich Cathedral on 29 July 1752.
² [Mason was then in Cambridge.]
³ The Rev. John Skynner, Fellow of St John's, elected Public Orator at Cambridge, 26 October 1752. He resigned in 1762.
⁴ The other candidate was John Ross, also Fellow of St John's, afterwards Bishop of Exeter. He was successful against Hurd for the Preachership of the Rolls.

M.ʳ W[arburton] and I laughed at your account of C.'s⁵ persecuting letters. They will certainly be printed and, it may be said, will do your fame at least as much service as the fond encomiums of F. For both these however I truly pity you. Was not Pope in the right when he preferred a fool's hate to his love?

As to the faithful Shepherdess,⁶ the event, as you say, turns out much to the credit of my divining faculty, the happinefs of which arises not from my superior knowledge of the town and the world, as you jestingly put it, but from my acquaintance with Garrick's ill taste, and foible as an actor. He is entre nous nothing when he is not playing tricks & shewing attitudes, for which you and Fletcher left him little room. M.ʳ W[arburton] abuses him for this folly. By the way you must send

⁵ [It may be inferred that "C.'s persecuting letters" and "the fond encomiums of F." were concerned with Mason's tragedy *Elfrida*, which had been published in March 1752. A note of Richard Hurd's identifies C. as Comber (probably William Comber, Fellow of Jesus). Nothing is known of the letters. Above "F." Fletcher is pencilled. This is an obvious mistake (see n. 6) and the identity of F. is revealed by a letter of Hurd's to Balguy, of 26 April 1762, in which he writes: "D.ʳ Barnard, of Eton, sent me the other day a new book by that Foster, who wrote a simple thing on Elfrida (Kilvert, p. 85). John Foster, B.A. 1753, was a Fellow of King's. He became an assistant master at Eton, and in 1765 succeeded Barnard as Master of the Upper School.]

⁶ On 26 Sept. 1752 Hurd had written to Balguy from Cambridge: "You will find Mason here, who talks of fitting up his *Faithful Shepherdess*, as being in some apprehension that Boyce and Garrick will force it from him". [From the reference to Fletcher a few lines below it may be inferred that Mason had been adapting the *Faithful Shepherdess* of John Fletcher, with a view to its production by Garrick at Covent Garden. The mention of Boyce (who had written the music for Mason's *Installation Ode* in 1749) suggests that it was intended to be a masque with music. There is one other allusion to the work. Mason, writing to Lord Nuneham, on 10 Nov. 1758, says: "The 'Faithful Shepherdess' is still untranscrib'd, and I have no curate now to do such things for me" (*Harcourt Papers*, vii, p. 10). Nothing more is known of it.]

him your MSS when he comes to town which will be in lefs than a fortnight. I saw Garrick last night in his element, playing *Jaffier* with Mofsop whom the town admires in *Pierre*. Write like Otway[7] and you will please. But when you do this, you will at least lose one of your admirers.

I have a deal to say to you on this head and on another of more importance. Have nothing to do with a great Lord in the North.[8] You shall know my reasons when I see you. I have so wretched a pen that writing is uneasy to me. All that you and I want to learn is to be content with a little and then we may be happier than great men, falsely so called, can make us.

All at Prior Park[9] sincerely esteem you. I cannot be more than I am,

Dearest Sir,

Your affectionate friend & serv.

R. HURD

You must direct to M. Brown[10] at Carlisle in Cumberland.

---

[7] Jaffier and Pierre are characters in Otway's *Venice Preserved*, which, produced in 1682, remained very popular all through the eighteenth century. Mossop is Henry Mossop (1729–75), an actor of great talent, but ruined by his vanity. Some contemporary critics compared him favourably with Garrick.

[8] Mason annotated this: "Lord Rockingham to whom some of my friends (without my knowledge) had recommended me. M." [For a fuller account of this see Warburton's letter to Hurd, of 9 May 1752, *Letters*, p. 78.]

[9] The residence, near Bath, of Mr Ralph Allen.

[10] [The Rev. John Brown (afterwards Dr), frequently referred to in the Letters (see L. VIII, n. 4), at this time held a small living near Carlisle.]

V

HURD *to* Mason

Camb. 20 Jan. 1753

Dear Sir

I suppose you have judged hardly of me for neglecting your letter of the 31st past all this time. But I have a Clerical excuse. I have been preparing for W[hite] Hall.[1] And when I set upon this work of sermonizing, I am in such impatience to get over it that I don't care to be interrupted by other matters. But I am now at liberty again and shall dedicate the first moments of my leisure to your service.

For news, there is little stirring, unless that our cause of Appeals[2] is expected to come to a hearing next month. I wish we may succeed. And yet 'tis certain that we, I mean the University, do not deserve succeſs. The greater part, as you know, oppose their own reasonable liberty, and the rest, excepting a very few, are ashamed

[1] Dr Sherlock, Bishop of London, appointed Hurd Cambridge Preacher at Whitehall Chapel in May 1750.
[2] [For two years the University was engaged in a bitter controversy concerning the Right of Appeal from the Vice-Chancellor's decision on questions of discipline. In March 1752 the Lord Chancellor, the Archbishop of Canterbury and others had been requested to act as referees and to decide the dispute. Hurd was apparently expecting them to meet and hear arguments on either side. But as the feelings that had been aroused subsided, tranquillity was restored without the referees taking any action. See D. A. Winstanley, *The University of Cambridge in the Eighteenth Century*, pp. 204 ff. In the heat of the controversy there had been a war of anonymous pamphlets. Hurd himself wrote *The Opinion of an Eminent Lawyer concerning the Right of Appeal from the Vice-Chancellor of Cambridge to the Senate*. Powell, Balguy and Mason also upheld the Right of Appeal, and other pamphlets were doubtfully attributed to their authorship. See C. Wordsworth, *Social Life at the English Universities in the Eighteenth Century*, pp. 617 ff.]

to appear in the vindication of it. You have one[3] in your eye, I dare say, whom it much more concerned, than it did me, to aſsert this cause, and who yet was afraid of being thought to aſsert it. He is lately charged however with the obnoxious Fragment.[4] The Bishops of Ely[5] and Chester[6] openly charged him with it. I told him so. And yet he took no method to clear himself either to them or others. Is not this mysterious? Is he grown indifferent, at last, to his good name? Or is he fearful of giving offence tho' in his own just support? All he has done has been to preach at St Mary's in praise of Candour[7] which he thinks sadly violated in our times by that outrageous resentment which all men are so forward to entertain against vice and vitious men. But all this I say to you *sub sigillo silentii et amicitiæ.*

This last word very luckily connects with what I have next to say to you. You want to hear how our friend's Sermons are relish'd at Cambridge. Why just as you might suppose. Either groſsly abused, or faintly commended. Roſs is clamorous against them: And a friend of yours,[8] whose *taste* is almost as squeamish as his *faith*, joins with him. There

---

[3] Qu. Mʳ Powell [H].

[4] [*A Fragment*, published in 1750, was one of the most scurrilous and effective of the pamphlets produced by the controversy. It is not known who was the author: but Powell's name does not seem to be mentioned in connexion with it elsewhere. See Wordsworth, *op. cit.* p. 621.]

[5] Sir Thomas Gooch, Master of Gonville and Caius College.

[6] Edmund Keene, Master of Peterhouse.

[7] The sermon (preached in the University Church) does not appear among *Dr Powell's Discourses*, edited by Balguy.

[8] Richard Hurd, junior, notes that this is George Ashby, the antiquary, of St John's College; afterwards its President.

13

is, on the other hand, a junto of friends who like some things but object to others as not accurate enough and metaphysical. Most agree to censure the *Style* and verily think, Mr W. writes worse & worse. Rofs was very gay some time since at my room on this last topic but unhappily for proof quoted a pafsage which I told him was, in my apprehension, incomparably the most excellent in the whole Volume. It is that (if you have the Sermons by you) about the *African Eloquence*:[9] a pafsage, the exquisite beauty of which these wretches may well be excused, if they never understand. One of their outcries, as usual, is against *subtleties and Refinements*. In relation to which I will transcribe what Mr W. wrote to me the other day,[10] to whom I had mentioned this stale objection. His answer is just and, in his manner, severe and witty: "*If an Afs could speak, he would call rose leaves such, that pafs over his palate unfelt; while he was at his substantial diet of good brown Thistles*". For my own opinion, if you have seen this volume yourself, I need not give it you. If you have not, I will only say they are the only model of Sermons hitherto published. I am not sure if the cavillers, I have spoken of, have the sense to see their excellencies. If they have, the worst thing I wish may befall their malignity in difsembling it, is the Imprecation of the Poet,[11] in truth a very severe one, *Virtutem videant intabescantque relictâ*. And with this punishment on their heads I leave them.

[9] See Warburton, *Principles of Natural and Revealed Religion* (*Works*, IV, p. 583).
[10] *Letters from a late Eminent Prelate*, No. LI, pp. 94 f., dated Prior Park, 15 Jan. 1753.
[11] Persius, *Satires*, 3, 38.

But I have something a little more serious to say to you. The excefsive ill usage, which the only great man of our times (for such he is, let fools & knaves say what they will to the contrary) is constantly receiving, kindles my Indignation, and so, I'm sure, it does your's. This has put a thing into my head, which per-haps, if I have health and spirits, I may sometime execute. The general plan is such as I have no great doubt of your liking. At least it flatters my Imagina-tion, at this distance, not a little. The design is so laid that it will give me the opportunity of defending any part of M.ʳ W.'s writings and character and yet in a way that will not be controversial nor, if well executed (of which I have the most reason to doubt) offensive to the delicacy ev'n of *Roseleaf* eaters. But of this pro-ject[12] I say no more at present, nor ever shall, unlefs it be executed, and then, perhaps, to no mortal but your-self. In the mean time, let this general Intimation sleep with you.

What you write of Garnet[13] is very contemptible. But no matter, let him exult in his good fortune. You and I, I verily believe, shall never envy Him. Or if you have any tendency that way, what will you give me for a *Charm* that will secure you from all danger. I picked it up in an old Ware-house, or rather Lumber-room of cast off goods, and yet there is no *Amulet* of

[12] It adds to the deliberateness of the tractate *On the Delicacy of Friendship*, which was not finished until 25 Nov. 1755, that nearly two years before Hurd was contemplating such a vindication of Warburton.

[13] [The reference is to John Garnett, Fellow of Sidney, author of a *Commentary on the Book of Job*, who in 1751 went to Ireland as chaplain to the Duke of Dorset, the Lord-Lieutenant. In August 1752 he was promoted to the united bishoprics of Leighton and

modern date and construction more serviceable. Guefs now if you can, from whose honest & plain-dealing pen these Rhymes have been dropped.

Fortune[14] is stately, solemne, proude, & hye,
   And Richefse geveth, to have servyce therefore;
The nedy Begger catcheth an half-peny;
   Some manne a thousande pounde, some lefse, some more.
   But for all that she keepeth ever in store
      From every manne some parcelle of his wyll
      That He maye pray therefore & serve her styll.

See here the tricks of this sly Goddefs, told in honest sense by this rude Enditer. But can you direct me to better sense in sprucer English? I trow not. However, let us weigh the matter. Your Bishop would say "Let *fortune* be as great a baggage, as she will, still She is better than *Poverty*: of all Spectres let me keep clear of this". Shall we subscribe to this so Episcopal determination, or shall we fetch counsel again from my old Oracle?

Ferns. Mason's feeling about his preferment was expressed in an epigram, a copy of which is in Mason's manuscript *Commonplace Book*, with a note that it was published in the *London Evening Post*:

On a late ecclesiastical promotion
Says Old Cam to the Bp, my Son is it so,
Is the Conge d'Elire sign'd, are you sure you shall go?
What! must Ireland enjoy all that genius and knowledge?
By my soul thoudst ha' made a rare head of a College.
"Sir, his Grace was so pressing a speedy translation,
Besides is cocksure from my next dedication."
Well, Jack! I begin now to smoak thy discernment,
Yet faith I beleivd eer thou got this preferment
That thy hunting so long had quite emptied thy fob
And in all senses made thee as poor as thy Job.]
[14] Sir Thomas More, Prologue to *The Boke of the fayre Gentylwoman, that no man shulde put his truste or confydence in, that is to say, Lady Fortune*: Stanza 36, "Fortune is stately..."; Stanza 22, "Poverte that of her gyftes...".

16

Povertee that of Her [Fortune's] gifts wyl nothynge take
    With mery cheere looketh upon the Prefse,
And seeth how fortune's householde goeth to wrecke
    "Fast by her standethe the wyse Socrates"[15]
    Aristippus, Pythagoras, and many a lease
        Of old Philosophers: And eke agaynst the Sonne
        Bakyth him poore Diogenes in his Tonne.

And so goeth on enumerating many poor but happy philosophers, from which number however I would willingly have you exempt, whatever may be the fate of one, who yet in all fortunes thinks he cannot fail of being, Dear Sir, Your faithful

and affectionate friend & Servt

R. HURD

VI

HURD *to* Mason

Dear Sir,

I write a few lines, rather because you seem to expect it of me, than that I have anything of consequence enough to make up a letter.

I had scarcely begun to reconcile myself to the bad news, I had received from Hull,[1] before I was attacked from another quarter, and in the most sensible manner; I mean with the report of poor Mr Horton's death, which happen'd suddenly, in one of those fits to

---

[15] [Opposite this line Hurd wrote in the margin: this verse done *en critique*.]

[1] See Kilvert, p. 50: in a letter to Balguy, Cambridge, 27 Sept. 1753, Hurd records the apparently contagious fever which caused the death of William Mason, senior, Vicar of Holy Trinity, Hull (August 26), and of two servants, and the illness of his widow. He asks Balguy to write to Mason, junior. "Anything from a friend on these occasions carries some comfort with it." [See also Gray's letter to Mason, 21 Sept. 1753, Tovey, I, p. 236.]

which he had, for some time, been subject.[2] You did not know Him, and, as it happens, it is very well you did not. For he was, without exception, the most amiable young man, I ever knew, and had a kind of fascination in his behaviour, which won upon all his acquaintance in a wonderful manner. It is some time since the qualities of the head have had but the second, and indeed a very subordinate place with me in my estimation of those few friends, whose acquaintance I care to cultivate. But the person, I speak of, had united these, in a high degree, with the most engaging temper I have ever met with. So that, on all accounts, I cannot but feel his loss very sensibly.—I have been reading much of late in a very contemplative author ('tis Bishop Butler) of this life's being a state of moral discipline and probation. I every day, more and more, find it to be so. And perhaps it is the best use, which our continuance in such a wretched world as this can serve to. You see by this the temper I write in and how much it needs the correction of that discipline, which the various accidents of life are perpetually furnishing. But not to trouble you with these uneasy reflexions, which what has lately befallen yourself must have given but too much room for, let me only say I shall be glad to see you here very soon and much more, if you return to us with those good spirits which you so rightly endeavour to keep up under all your distreſses.

    You will find all your friends here except Mʳ Gray,[3]

----

[2] Richard Hurd, junior, notes in pencil: "Mʳ Edward Horton was of Emman. Coll. He was son of Christopher Horton Esq. of Catton in Derbyshire, whose eldest daughter, Frances, was married to Sir Edward Littleton (Hurd's pupil) in 1752".
[3] [By this time Hurd must have been acquainted with Gray.]

who, as you would hear from himself, was called away, immediately on his coming hither, by the illnefs of a near Relation.[4] I gave M.ʳ Warburton some account of you, when I wrote last. At all times believe me,

Dear Sir

Your affectionate humble

Serv.ᵗ

Cambridge   R. HURD
22 Oct. 1753

VII

HURD *to* Mason

Dear Sir

For you who

"In Chiswick Bow'rs your easy hours employ"[1]

not to find time to give me a letter is very inexcusable. And if I knew in what way to do it, I should certainly punish you as you deserve. Perhaps the best revenge I can take will be to teaze you into the remembrance of your old friends, if nothing else will do it.

I understand from D.ʳ N.[2] that Dodsley is not over-

---

[4] [On October 18 Gray wrote from Stoke Poges to Thomas Wharton: "as soon as I arrived at Cambridge, I found a letter informing me my Aunt Rogers had had a stroke of the Palsy, so that I stay'd only a single day, & set out for this place". Tovey, I, p. 241.]

[1] [Mason was domestic chaplain to the Earl of Holdernesse, who for some years "rented a small villa at Chiswick" (Mason, *Works*, I, p. 97 n.). Mason was there at this time (Tovey, I, p. 284). Hurd's reference to "Chiswick Bow'rs" was probably suggested by Mason's *Elegy addressed to Miss Pelham on the death of her father*, which was written in 1754 (*Works*, I, p. 97):
"Where D'Arcy call'd to Chiswick's social bower
   Mild mirth, and polish'd ease, and decent joy".]

[2] Mr Thomas Nevile jocosely called Dr [H]. See L. II, n. 5.

fond of engaging in this second Imitation.[3] I suppose
he is very right in believing that it will not sell. And
yet worse things sell every day. It is true, the sort of
writing does not suit the D.[r] perfectly. Besides other
defects, he neither thinks nor speaks exactly enough to
excell in the Horatian manner. Yet in all things he has
attempted in this way there are pretty things enough,
one would think, to carry off a six penny pamphlet.
But betwixt a want of curiosity and of taste in this our
age, an obscure writer has a bad time of it.

You are to know that, as I have no expectation of
entertainment from the wits of these days, I mean now
you have burnt your Lyre,[4] I am content to seek it in
the past ages. And as I know not why I have always
conceiv'd high things of the Italian poets, I have been
lately trying to get some acquaintance with them.
Tho' I cannot boast of having made any great pro-
grefs in them, I see enough to convince me that they
are above every thing which is call'd poetry in the other
modern languages, except perhaps in our own, which

[3] [Dodsley had published in March 1755 *The First Satire of the
First Book of Horace Imitated*; and in February 1756 he published
The Seventeenth Epistle of the First Book, and in April *The Eighteenth
Epistle of the First Book*. These were anonymous.] In 1758 Nevile
published, over his own name, his *Imitations of Horace*, which included his separate publications. The book was dedicated to Hurd.
" I had", he says, "too great an interest in the use of your name to
suffer this opportunity to escape me without acknowledging my
connections with one, who has it in his power to recommend a
work of this kind to the public by his life, no less than his writings ".

[4] [The allusion to Mason's having burnt his Lyre is explained
by Warburton's letter to Hurd of 24 Oct. 1754 (*Letters*, p. 125).
Before Mason was ordained he called upon Warburton, who im-
pressed upon him that he ought not to go into orders unless he
had a resolution "to dedicate all his studies to the service of religion, and totally to abandon his poetry". Mason agreed that
this sacrifice was required of him, but it was not long before he
resumed his poetical efforts.]

I am us'd to prefer before all others for the force of colouring and height of Invention. Or if this be a prejudice, it is not, I think, to affirm that the french poetry is the tamest poorest thing in the world in comparison of the Italian. One thing that created a presumption in favour of this last, was the observing that Italy was the School to our own poets, and indeed writers of all sorts, at the time when they were the best. It is plain that Milton owed almost as much to the Tuscan as the Greek poets. In short I'm grown on the sudden such an inamorato of these Italian Bards, that I can almost bear their Sonnets. Yet I wonder that, when they have so many better things to value themselves upon, they should lay such a strefs on this elegant indeed, but trifling form of composition. I suspect the folly might arise from a wrong interpretation of the famous maxim *Difficilia quæ pulchra*, which says only that *excellent things are difficult*, whereas they seem to have taken the matter the other way and to have gone on the supposition, that *difficult things are always excellent*; a maxim, which for anything I know might set the discarded french dancers above the best poets.

I reverence that great critic M.ʳ Dodsley prodigiously for his sagacious conjectures about the author of a late pamphlet.[5] However, I agree with you that Jortin did not deserve the honour of this ridicule. And I'm persuaded, whoever the writer was, that he was betrayed into it by the weakest of all our pafsions, an inordinate friendship: In short the very same which makes me

[5] Hurd's pamphlet *On the Delicacy of Friendship*, dated "Lincoln's Inn, 25 Nov. 1755", had just appeared. [See Warburton, *Letters*, p. 150. It was anonymous and Dodsley had doubtless suggested to Mason that Hurd was the author.]

run on at this strange rate and pester you with so long
a letter, when I might well have sav'd both you and
myself that trouble by leaving you to guefs how entirely I am always,

Dear Sir,

Your affectionate friend and Servant

Camb.   R HURD
31 Dec. 1755

VIII

HURD *to* Mason

Dear Sir,

I have your favour of yesterday. And to show you
how punctual a correspondent I am, I mean to those
for whom I profefs an *inordinate*[1] friendship (for as to
others, I afsure you, I trouble them as little in this way
as any body) I will make my acknowledgments to you
for it directly.

As to N.'s[2] affair, I will break it to him the first
opportunity and will let you know his resolution.

With regard to the letters to D.[3], I can readily believe that they are written with a franknefs which to
such a man might have been spar'd. But I think there

[1] [Hurd is repeating the phrase that he used in the last paragraph of his preceding letter.]
[2] [Richard Hurd notes that Nevile (see L. II, n. 5) is meant, but
the allusion is not explained.]
[3] [As Richard Hurd noted "D." is Robert Dodsley, "A." Ralph
Allen of Prior Park and "a friend of his" is Warburton who had
married his niece. It may be inferred that Dodsley had proposed
to publish something, which Warburton considered offensive to
himself. Dodsley's brother, Isaac, was gardener to Mr Allen and
on that account, Hurd thinks, Robert Dodsley should not have
had any hand in the publication. Warburton, or one of his friends,
had written to Dodsley, who seems to have consulted Mason, who
"gave him good advice".]

22

is great reason in what he says. You know D.'s brother is Mr A.'s servant. And on that account, if on no other, Dodsley should have declin'd having any hand in publishing an abuse on a friend of his, and one of his family. I think you gave him good advice, and I suppose he will take it.

You don't tell me if you have seen Dr Brown.[4] He is in his old lodgings in Tavistock Street. Athelstan[5] comes on pretty early in the next month. Mr B.[6] and I expect him here one of these days, and then we are to sit upon it. But the D.^r is either so lazy or so carelefs himself, and Garrick[7] is so peremptory in having everything his own way, that no great good, I foresee, will come of our criticisms, if they should be ever so reasonable. However the poet may wing his flight for *Gain*, not glory; and if so, it is no great matter, provided it pafses upon the Stage, what the few in the closet think of his performance.

I really think, from the little I have seen, that the Italian poets are excellent. They have false thoughts and affected conceits in abundance, it is true. But

[4] John Brown, of St John's College; D.D. 1755 [best known as the author of *The Estimate*]. "Mr Browne", wrote Warburton on 30 Jan. 1749–50 (*Letters*, p. 27), "has fine parts...and...a force of versification very uncommon." For "our friend, little Browne's" opinion of Hurd see *Letters*, p. 104: "a man who sees by an early penetration that which the generality never find out till they have drudged on to the end of life". [Mason did not like Brown. Gray writing to Mason in 1757 alludes to "your enemy Dr Brown." Tovey, I, p. 350.]

[5] *Athelstan*, a tragedy, by Dr Brown, 8vo, was produced at Covent Garden on 27 Feb. 1756. Garrick played in it and wrote an epilogue; Nichols, *op. cit.* II, p. 286.

[6] Thomas Balguy [H]. See *Introduction*, p. xxii, n. 18.

[7] For Garrick's part in Brown's previous play, *Barbarossa*, acted 17 Dec. 1754, and published by Bowyer that month, see Nichols, *op. cit.* II, p. 275.

their allegorical fiction and the brightnefs of their imagery, the efsentials of poetry, make us ample amends for these defects. The french poets are chast and correct. But their invention is poor and their fancies prosaic. One thing is remarkable enough. Tho' the Italians are sometimes, nay frequently affected, they have, in general, a simplicity which is charming. Don't you think it extraordinary that Milton, notwithstanding the bad taste of his age here at home, and these constant conceits that deform his models, the Italian poets, should yet keep so clear of all these affectations? I can't but look upon this circumstance as a singular proof of the vast superiority of his genius. You'll think from my saying so much of this subject, that I am quite wild about the Italian poetry. You would think so much more if I was to tell you that I have ev'n gone so far myself as to write a sonnet.[8]

[8] The sonnet is written out in the Bishop's *Commonplace Book*, II, p. 253, from which it is here copied:

Mason, M^r. A Sonnet address'd to him on his leaving College and going into the family of Lord Holdernesse—

To Mr Mason.

Was it for this insidious friendship strove
  To clasp our bosoms in it's silken snare,
  For this, Thy virtues bloom'd so wondrous fair,
And Fame for Thee th' unfading chaplet wove?

Say, will yon Linnet from her Spray remove
  Where sportive She and free from ev'ry care
  Warbles at will her softly-soothing air,
And for the glitt'ring cage desert the grove?

Then may'st Thou, sweetest of the tuneful quire
  Thy gentle Muse, the lov'd and loving friend,
    The golden competence, the vacant hour,

Celestial blefsings, barter for the hire
  Of witlings base, and thy free soul descend
    To toil for unblefs'd gold, and flatter pow'r.
                R. H. 3 Jan. 1756.

I know you laugh at my folly. But your revenge upon me shall go no further: the rather because, to tell you a secret, you are the subject of it. For you grow so captious, if one offers to give you a little advice (and this sonnet is altogether monitory or rather vituperative) that, after your treatment of my well-intended dialogue,[9] you may be sure I shall avoid this route for the future.

I was very well pleas'd with your *Divine* and *Pretty*

The sonnet, it would seem, was too "monitory" or "vituperative" for Mason, and his relations with his noble patron might have been strained by phrases like "the hire of witlings base". On the same page of his *Commonplace Book*, Hurd added a revised version, which is headed: "Afterwards, alter'd into the following, corrected by M.r Mason himself":

> A gentle *Linnet* debonnair and gay
> Whilom had rov'd the wood in careless vein,
> Perch'd where it pleas'd, and with it's honey'd strain
> Had wak'd the Morn and clos'd the eye of Day.
>
> A *Fowler* heard, and o'er her custom'd spray
> Inwove of liméd twigs the tangling train
> And with her fav'rite food bestrew'd the plain:
> The wiry cage unseen at distance lay.
>
> Blythe and unweeting to the charmed Tree
> The Songster comes, and claps his little wing,
> Then downward bends to peck the golden fare.
>
> Will no kind hand the struggling captive free?
> He yields to fate: he droops: forgets to sing.
> Nor greets his Lord with one sweet-warbled air.

[The reference in Hurd's title to Mason's "leaving College and going into the family of Lord Holdernesse" is not easy to explain in connexion with the date "3 Jan. 1756", at which it was written. Mason, according to his own statement (see above, p. xxx), was "instituted to the Living of Aston and appointed Chaplain to the Earl of Holdernesse in November 1754", and he had been in attendance on his patron throughout 1755. In December 1755 his year of grace as a Fellow of Pembroke College ran out, and by continuing to hold the living, he would have to vacate his fellowship. His decision to do so meant that he was severing his connexion with Cambridge and this may have been in Hurd's mind. See L. XI, n. 2.]

[9] [See L. XI, n. 3.]

Gentleman's opinion of a late pamphlet.[10] For if the Irony be too fine for the one, and not fine enough for the other, it is likely to be in that middle way, in which the author, I should suppose, intended to write it. But don't conclude from my saying thus much that I have any peculiar tendernefs for this namelefs offspring. I don't so much as tell you my conjectures. For the knowing ones here pretend to fix the parent, nay to swear to him by certain lineaments which, for anything I know, may be as familiar to you as any other. You don't meddle with Greek in town. Otherwise I could tell you of an awful grammarian who decrees that the concluding Sentence[11] is not to be found in the *Cyropædia* nor in *Leed's Lucian,* and therefore as he believes in no genuine Greek writer whatsover. So that the author is likely to have the name, tho' of writing an indifferent pamphlet, yet of composing good Greek, which at least will recommend him to the favour of great Scholars.

I say nothing in excuse of all this prate but that I am very truly and affectionately

Your's

Camb.   R. HURD
8 Jan. 1756

---

[10] *On the Delicacy of Friendship.*
[11] [Hurd refers to suggestions made by "persons to whom I communicated the design of this addrefs", and the pamphlet ends with a passage which the author professes to have heard quoted by "one of these rhetorical declaimers. He did not say where he found it, and you would not like it the better if he had, but as I remember it, it was delivered in these words: Ἐμοὶ πρὸς φιλο-σόφους ἐστὶ φιλία· πρὸς μέντοι σοφιστὰς ἢ γραμματιστὰς, ἢ τοιοῦτο γένος ἕτερον ἀνθρώπων κακοδαιμόνων οὔτε νῦν ἐστὶ φιλία μήτε ὕστερον πότε γένοιτο".]

IX

HURD *to* Mason

Dear Sir,

I send you a letter from Dr Macro.[1] I have just now receiv'd one from P.P.[2] in which there is a Paragraph relating to you. I transcribe it with the more pleasure because it confirms the judgment which you know I have always pafsed upon your Poetry.

Mr Mason was so kind to send us his Odes.[3] They fully support and maintain his character. And this is no slight or vulgar commendation, when it is the common fate of his contemporaries to have ev'ry last production below the preceding. In a word, they charm me much. That on Melancholly[4] is my favourite. You said truly: He compliments his Patron artfully and decently.[5] It is of importance to a man's excelling that he should understand his *fort*, early. The Ode is certainly our Friend's. And if he will indulge himself in Poetry; that is the Province he ought to cultivate. There will be many favourable circumstances, besides his Genius, attending. I will mention only one, That great Repertory of poetical subjects of the Lyric kind, as well as poetical Images, the Bible.

Let me hear from You and let me know which of your court Admirers makes you the happiest compliment.

Your's very affectionately

R. HURD

Camb. 3 Apr. 1756

[1] Rev. Cox Macro, D.D., antiquary; befriended Hurd during his curacy in Norfolk; see above, L. I, n. 1.
[2] Prior Park; Warburton was there at the time; *Letters*, I, p. 154; but the letter quoted is not included there.
[3] Published by Dodsley, 15 March 1756.
[4] Ode vii, *To a Friend*, Mason, *Works*, I, pp. 42 f.
[5] Ode vi, *To Independency*, Mason, *Works*, I, pp. 38 ff.

X

Hurd *to* Mason

Camb. 16 June 1756

Dear Sir,

Your favour of the 8th came hither the day after I was set out on a journey into Norfolk, from which I am but just now return'd. I mention this because I should otherwise have acquainted you that Dr W. is in town, where he has been ever since the beginning of the month. I think you will do well to write to him immediately.

The public taste has shewn itself to be what I have long thought it, by its reception of your Odes. It has been so viciated by this long run of insipid Romances that nothing manly or great is at all relish'd. A little easy sing-song, intermixd with what they call *Sentiment*, is the utmost that common readers have any idea of. The sublimest poetry is as unintelligible to them as Coptic. In short, you come too late by half a century to give that pleasure you might reasonably expect to have given, by the finest Odes we have any example of in our language. However, the few will still have a juster way of thinking, and to these a good writer must now be content to write to.

I must have a high idea of a young man [Mr Burke[1]] that could imitate L. B. so perfectly.[2] But I must still

---

[1] [The name is inserted above the line in Hurd's handwriting.]
[2] Edmund Burke's *Vindication of Natural Society* was published in May 1756. Cf. John Morley, *Burke*, p. 13: "Excellent judges of style made sure that the writing was really Bolingbroke's, and serious critics of philosophy never doubted that the writer, whoever he was, meant all that he said".

think his Imitation a bad *Irony*. Had the author intended only, in the character of *Sophist*, to mimic Lord Bolingbroke's style and manner and to compose a tract that should pass for his, I should have called it a happy and most ingenious forgery. But an *Ironist* has quite another office. His busineſs is, *to imitate so as to expose*. When he attempts his *manner*, and much more when he adopts his *principles*,[3] he should take care by a constant exaggeration to make the *ridicule* shine through the Imitation. Whereas this *Vindication* is everywhere enforc'd, not only in the language, and on the principles of L. Bol., but with so apparent, or rather so real an earnestneſs, that half his purpose is sacrificed to the other. One sees it extremely *like*, but the likeneſs is not such as excites *ridicule*. 'Tis true, a good Ironist will exaggerate so discretely that all he says may seem not improbably to come from the *person represented*. And when a work of this sort is so manag'd, we call it a *delicate Irony*. But to personate another witht any exaggeration or with so little as to escape notice, may be thought a *delicacy* indeed, but gives one a strange notion of an *Irony*. In short, if the writer meant to expose Lord Bol. by an *ironical application of his principles*,[4] he has mifs'd his aim, for he has only rais'd an admiration of his own talents. If he thought the most *serious application of his principles* sufficient to expose him

<hr>

[3] [The text is given as Hurd wrote it. It has been corrected, apparently in Mason's hand, to read as follows: "When he adopts the manner, and much more when he adopts the principles of another, he should take care . . . to make his ridicule shine, etc."]

[4] Cf. Morley, *op. cit.* p. 15. "It is a satirical literary handling of the great proposition which Burke enforced, with all the thunder and lurid effulgence of his most passionate rhetoric, five and thirty years later."

he has judgd wrong, for as extravagant as his conclusion is, one is half convinc'd of it by his premises.
The *Vindication* requires an answer as much, perhaps
will not admit so easy an answer, as the *fragments &
Efsays.*[5]

I am sorry I shall not see you in my pafsage next
week thro' London. I go from thence in the Stage-
coach and so shall not have it in my power to stop at
Tunbridge, if the road lies thro' it.

Believe me, Dear Sir,

Your most faithful & affectionate

R. HURD

At the foot of the letter Mason has added this
comment:

My correspondent was nearly guilty of the same fault,
when he wrote his first Dialogue.[6] The Irony was so fine that
several readers thought it a grave & serious vindication of
Insincerity. M.

XI

HURD *to* Mason

Brighthelmstone, 7 Aug. 1756

Dear Mr Mason

I did not care to press you to a journey, which I
doubted would not be very agreable to you, but we
were much disappointed at not seeing you, especially

[5] [In 1754 Mallet had published Bolingbroke's collected works,
which included *Essays addressed to Alexander Pope* and *Fragments or
Minutes of Essays.* To these Hurd must be referring.]

[6] *On Sincerity in the Commerce of the World*: between Dr Henry
More and Edmund Waller, Esq. 1759.

after M.[r] Noble[1] had informed us that you certainly intended it. I should have been glad of your company for many reasons; amongst others that I might have known something more of the new scheme[2] you have enterd upon. I rejoyce with you on this project, not only because I dare say it is a good one, but because it will serve to fill up your time and employ your leisure very agreably. I cannot tell how you find it but the best part of my entertainment in this foolish world arises from my own thoughts, which, bad as they are, are a better amusement than any I find in what is called general conversation. Some of these I should perhaps have troubled you with, if I had seen you here. I told you of my Political Dialogue.[3] It runs out into two parts, each of them pretty long, but the subject, at least if I don't spoil it in the handling, not uninteresting. The first of these is quite finished, I mean thrown completely into form, so that I might

[1] [Mr Noble, who is mentioned also in the concluding sentence of this letter, may have held some post in the household of Earl Holdernesse. See Gray's letter to Mason of 19 Dec. 1756 (Tovey, I, p. 311.]
[2] [Richard Hurd in a pencil note to this letter explains Mason's "new scheme" as "going in to the family of Lord Holdernesse", perhaps taking the phrase from the title of his uncle's Sonnet to Mason (see L. VIII, n. 8). But Hurd could not at the date of this letter be alluding to this as a "new scheme", nor does his description suggest the duties of a domestic chaplain. The project which "will serve to fill up your time and employ your leisure" was more probably the composition of Mason's tragedy, *Caractacus*, to which Hurd refers below. Two months before Gray wrote to Mason: "I rejoice to know that the genial influences of the spring . . . have hatched high and unimaginable fantasies in you" and Mason explained this in a note (*Memoirs*, p. 246): "I had sent him my first idea of Caractacus drawn out in a short argument".]
[3] The *Dialogues* were not published till 1759, and the authorship of them was only acknowledged in the preface to the third edition, 1764.

have taken your judgment of it. I must now be contented to wait till we meet next winter at Cambridge, by which time I hope to have finished the remainder, which is to finish all that I intend of this nature. If you get Caractacus[4] in the same forwardneſs I promise to repay your criticism, not with the dull civility current among authors but with the free censure of one that takes a greater interest in what you write than in any trash of his own.

I suppose you would learn from Dr Warb[5] that he leaves Durham immediately after the 13th inst. So that you will hardly pay the visit you designd him. You are very kind in your wishes that I may find the full benefit of this Sea-Regimen. I dare not promise myself too much from it. I remember those oracular lines of Pope:[6]

The young disease that must prevail at length
Grows with his growth and strengthens with his strength.

It is enough if I can but palliate a disorder which comes, like all our woe, by inheritance. Happy! if I but inherited the integrity of mind and serenity of temper which made it so easy to him from whom I derived it.[7] But I grow too grave even for you. Let me end by telling you that Mr Powell is here with his Sister. They came down on a visit to an Eſsex family that is here and I suppose will leave us again next week.

[4] Between *Caractacus* and the *Dialogues* there was something of a race for publication, though the pace was not furious. They both appeared in May 1759.

[5] [In March 1755 Warburton had been appointed to a prebend at Durham.]

[6] Pope wrote "subdue" (not "prevail"), *Essay on Man*, l. 135.

[7] [Hurd's father died in November 1755.]

M.ʳ Manwaring[8] sends compliments. If this finds you in Town, remember us both to M.ʳ Noble. Believe me most cordially,

Dear Sir

Your affectionate friend & Servant
R. HURD

XII

HURD *to* Gray[1]

Dear Sir, *7 Jan. 1757*[2]

I will beg the favour of your Milton[3] once more. I have considerd your Observations[4] in the Paper you oblig'd me with yesterday. I think them excellent and shall correct accordingly.

The only one of the least consequence which sticks

---

[8] [The Rev. John Mainwaring, who was at Brighthelmstone with Hurd, was Mason's contemporary at St John's, of which he was a Fellow. See L. LI, n. 5.]

[1] [In March 1756 Gray had migrated from Peterhouse to Pembroke College. Whenever his acquaintance with Hurd began (see L. III, n. 4, L. VI, n. 3), by the date of this letter they were on terms of intimate friendship.]

[2] The letter, dated at the end "Ēman: Friday morning", was sent by hand: "To M.ʳ Gray of Pembroke". A copy of the letter, which Hurd kept, is dated in his own hand: "7 Jan. 1757".

[3] [Gray had copies of *Paradise Lost* and *Paradise Regained* interleaved; in these he had transcribed passages from ancient and modern authors, "in which he observed a similitude of thought or expression". Hurd had borrowed the books for the dissertation referred to in n. 4.]

[4] Hurd noted in the margin of his copy: "on the Letter to M.ʳ Mason on the *Marks of Imitation.*" He was preparing a new edition of the two Literary Epistles of Horace: in this he included a dissertation, *On the Marks of Imitation,* in the form of a letter to Mason. (See L. XIV, n. 3.) It closed with a tribute of affection to Mason and to "those many years of friendship we have passed together in this place". "The coming years of my life (he was instituted to Thurcaston, 16 Feb. 1757) will not,

with me is your hint about the Introduction.[5] And I
owe it to your franknefs, to tell you my sincere sentiments. I hate the hypocrisy of those men who think
to cover their dullnefs under the mask of piety, as much
as you can do. I know too what is to be said for those
who have not devoted themselves to a Profefsion: And
still further for those who read the Poets, not for
amusement only, but to contend with the best of them.
I honour, in a word, true poetry and true Poets as
much as any body. And I think, in particular, with
you that M.r Pope's apologies for himself were very
needlefs. Yet still in my own case I must profefs to you
with sincerity, that what I say in the Letter is my real
opinion. The Profefsion, I am of, is a sacred one. And
tho' it does not oblige me to renounce the poets, my
businefs, I think, should lie elsewhere. I afsure you,
I take this design to be but a decent one in my circumstances, and, considering the circumstances of the
time, an absolute Duty. So that when these things are
out of my hands, and the few Dialogues I mention'd
to you, I have determin'd long since to pafs the re-

I foresee, in many respects, be what the past have been to me.
But, till they take me from myself, I must always bear about me
the agreeable remembrance of our friendship."
   [5] With a country parson's life in front of him, Hurd starts his
dissertation by reflecting that his "younger years" had been
devoted to the study of "poets of ancient and modern fame".
"But you, who love me so well, would not wish me to pafs
more of my life in these flowery regions.... Yet in saying this
I would not be thought to afsume that severe character; which,
though sometimes the garb of reason, is oftner, I believe, the mask
of dulnefs, or of something worse.... I may recollect with pleasure,
but must never live over again

     'Pieriosque dies, et amantes carmina somnos'"
                       [Statius, *Silvae*, i, 3, 23].

mainder of my Life (I mean if in that Remainder I do any thing as a writer) in the concerns of my own Profefsion. However there are some things in the Introduction put more strongly than they needed to have been, and these I shall soften; principally because what I leave will then be understood, not as words of course, but as my real meaning.

You will think I treat you very formally, in entering into this serious explanation. I do it to show you on what grounds, and with what reluctance, I deny myself the use of any part of your kind Intimations to me.

I am, Dear Sir,

Your very oblig'd humble Servant

* Em̄an:*   R. HURD
Friday morning

XIII

HURD *to* Gray

Dear Sir,   *[April ? 1757]*[1]

You want amusement at this time. I therefore take the liberty to inclose a translation of Aristotle's Ode, which I have thought of printing in the notes on Horace.[2] In the main it reads easily enough; but you will tell me what it wants of being to your mind. Mr̥

---

[1] [The letter—the cover of which, addressed "To Mr̥ Gray of Pembroke", shows that it was sent by hand—is not dated. There is a note of Richard Hurd's: "Suppose 1757", and the allusions to the edition of Horace make this certain. The opening words: "You want amusement at this time" may refer to the state of depression into which Gray was plunged early in the year (see Tovey, I, p. 327, n. 2.). April is a probable month.]

[2] See Hurd's *Q. Horatii Flacci Epistolæ ad Pisones ad Augustum*, the third edition, 1757, I, p. 159, where the Greek drinking song and the "elegant translation...from the same hand which has recently entertained us with some spirited imitations of Horace" are given. The allusion is to Nevile, see L. VII, n. 3.

35

3-2

Nevile was so good as to turn it for me, and I know will take a pleasure to correct it according to any hints you shall give him. I need not say that the Original is in Diog. Laertius and in the 15th book, I think, of the Athenæus.[3]

Dear Sir,
Your faithful humble Servant

Eman: Tuesday   R. HURD

XIV

HURD *to* Gray

Dear Sir

I give you many thanks for the favour of your Odes,[1] which I have received after a tedious expectation. You may be sure the title-page[2] amused us a good deal, but Mr Brown has explained it. It is not worth while to tell you how they are received here. But every body would be thought to admire. 'Tis true, I believe, the greater part don't understand them.

I have been amusing myself in my way, since you left us. The Letter to Mason[3] is printed off, and I

---

[3] [Diog. Laert. v, 5; Athenaeus xi, 57, p. 696, where it is argued that Aristotle's poem to Virtue is a drinking song and not a paean.]

[1] [Gray's *Odes*, the first book printed by Walpole at the Strawberry Hill Press, was published by Dodsley on 8 August 1757. On 25 July Gray wrote to James Brown (President of Pembroke College) that copies would be sent, which Brown was to give to Gray's friends in Cambridge. The names included Hurd, Balguy and Nevile. See Tovey, I, p. 341.]

[2] [The motto on the title-page was ΦΩΝΑΝΤΑ ΣΥΝΕΤΟΙΣΙ. As Gray wrote to Wharton on 17 August: "the great objection is obscurity, no body knows what we would be at...in short the Συνετοί appear to be still fewer, than even I expected". Tovey, I, p. 345.]

[3] [The "Letter to Mr Mason on the Marks of Imitation", dated "Camb. 15 Aug. 1757", was published separately and afterwards included in the edition of Horace.]

shall send you a copy very soon to Dodsley's. The dialogues[4] too are all finished after a sort; so that I shall have work enough for you against our next meeting in November. I should be better pleased, if you would find work for me. And I hope you don't forget, among your other amusements this summer, your design for a history of the English poetry.[5] You might be regulating your plan, and digesting the materials you have by you. I shall teaze you perpetually, till you set about the project in good earnest. It is a wonderful favourite with me, and will, I am certain, in your hands be a work of much use as well as elegance.

Mason has never once writ in all this time, which I

---

[4] [See L. XI, n. 3.]
[5] [In the *Advertisement* prefixed to his poem *The Fatal Sisters* (published in *Poems*, by Mr Gray, 1768) Gray wrote: "The Author once had thoughts (in concert with a Friend) of giving *the History of English Poetry*.... He has long since drop'd his design, especially after he had heard, that it was already in the hands of a Person well qualified to do it justice, both by his taste, and his researches into antiquity". The friend was Mason, to whom Warburton, in July 1752, had sent Pope's scheme for such a history. Gray's *Commonplace Book* contains material that he had collected for the purpose: some of which may be assigned to dates between 1755 and 1758. Walpole in a letter of 5 May 1761 refers to "The History of English bards which he and Mason are writing" (*Letters*, v, pp. 55–6). We do not know when the design was abandoned: the "Person well qualified to do justice" to the design was Thomas Warton.] To Warton on 14 Oct. 1762 Hurd wrote a letter (of which Hurd's own copy is still preserved at Hartlebury) thanking him for his *Observations on the Faery Queen*: "You have indeed taken the only way to penetrate the mysteries of Spenser's poetry, which is by investigating the manners & usages of Chivalry and Romance....And I will not despair of seeing the whole subject fully open'd & explained by you one day, if you persist, as I hope you will, in the noble design of giving a history, in form, of the English Poetry". For Hurd's later correspondence with Warton and Gray on this subject, see L. XXVI, n. 1.

take prodigiously ill, and desire you will tell him so. Dr Warburton sends me word too, he did not keep his appointment with him of going to Durham[6]. So that I can only conclude he is laid up of a fit of the Muse, or perhaps is gone to pay a visit to his Druids at Mona.

If you give me the pleasure of hearing from you, you must write very soon.[7] For I grow sick of this place, and set out on the 29.th on my summer rambles. It will be a satisfaction to hear that you are well. I am sollicitous for nothing else. For you can never want the best sort of amusements. Once more, let me thank you for the Odes, which I like the better upon every reading. Mr Nevile too desires me to make his acknowledgments in full form. He is mightily flatter'd with the present you was so kind to make him.

I am, Dear Sir,

Your very affectionate humble

Servant

Em̄an: Coll:
16 Aug. 1757

R. HURD

XV

HURD to Gray

Dear Sir,

Camb. 28 Aug. 1757

I write this to be conveyed to you by Mr Mason. We were together, when your favour of the 25.th arrived,

---

[6] Warburton (*Letters from a late eminent Prelate*, p. 183) wrote from Durham, 9 Aug. 1757: "Our friends M. and B. could not agree to come here in time; so they agreed not to come at all". [In the second edition, p. 249, the names "Mason and Browne" are printed in full. For Browne (sc. John Brown) see L. VIII, n. 4.]
[7] Gray's reply, dated Stoke, 25 Aug. 1757, was printed by Mason, *Memoirs*, p. 249. See Tovey, I, p. 346.

38

and laughed very heartily at the judgments of your great men and great women. Poor people, it is not for them to understand what you write. But without understanding, they will learn to admire, of their Betters. Every body here, that knows anything of such things, applauds the Odes. And the readers of Pindar dote upon them.

I am truly concerned for what you tell me of your indisposition. You must abstain from books for the present, and use all the exercise you can. I should fancy, if you took a Post-chaise and went to dine with Mason at Kensington,[1] it would be a relief to you. His Caractacus mends daily, and will come to good in the end, in spite of Lords and Ladies, who will not like it.

I set forward on my journey to morrow. If I find a day of leisure, or rather of *enui*, I may attempt to enliven it by writing to you again. In the mean time take care of your health and believe me,

Dear Sir,

Your very affectionate friend and

humble Servant

R. HURD

P.S. Mr Brown,[2] to whom I shew'd the paragraph in your Letter, sends compliments.

[1] [Mason had just been appointed Chaplain in Ordinary to King George the Second.]
[2] [In the postscript to his letter to Hurd of 25 Aug. Gray wrote: "If Mr Brown falls in your way, be so good to shew him, the beginning of this letter, and it will save me the labour of writing the same thing twice" (Tovey, I, p. 347).]

XVI

H U R D *to* Mason

P[rior] P[ark] 30 Nov. 1757

Dear Sir,

We have read over Caractacus together, and the enclosed brief notes, if you can read them, will let you into D.ʳ W.'s judgment of it. He lays an exceeding great strefs on the affair of human Sacrifices.[1] This is the main point. In every other respect, he applauds your play extremely. Thinks it will be a prodigiously fine thing, vastly above Elfrida.[2] You would probably have had all this and more, to greater advantage, under his own hand. But his businefs calls him away to Bristol,[3] and, to lose no time, I engaged to give you this hasty account of his censures, in his absence. I forgot to tell you, in the notes, that *Evelyne's* prayer of *One and All*[4] struck him exceedingly. Your Ode charms him. In short, everything is as I could wish. As to my own judgment, I agree in all the points here mentioned in the inclos'd papers. I have besides, it may be, some additional criticisms of my own to make. But I defer giving you this trouble, till I look it over

---

[1] See L. XVIII.

[2] Gray writes to Mason, 28 Sept. 1757 (Tovey, I, p. 354): "The contrivance, the manners, the interests, and the expression, go beyond the dramatic part of your Elfrida, many, many leagues".

[3] [Warburton had been appointed Dean of Bristol in September of this year.]

[4] *Caractacus* (Mason, *Works*, II, pp. 150 f.):

"Give her peace;
And, to endear it more, be that blest peace
Won by her brother's sword. Oh bless his arm,
And bless his valiant followers, one, and all".

with you, more at our leisure, in London. Your letter by to day's post prefses for it. And I shall send it with the books directly. I thank you for the receipt of the first fruits.

I have one word of advice, entirely from myself. I take for granted, you will not print this winter. I think you should keep it by you, one year more. So promising a thing, which will establish your reputation, should be quite perfect. For the like reason, I am not for your shewing it about till the Odes are finishd and inserted, and everything done to your satisfaction. I don't know whether Lord H[oldernefse] can be put off, I mean from shewing it directly where you said.[5] If he can, I should be glad. You see I am frank in my way. But I am so out of an extreme sollicitude for your reputation, and the credit of a play, which, when it has your last hand, will disgrace all the Athelstans[6] and Douglafses[7] of our times, to that degree, that no man will bear to hear of them. Let me hear from you very soon. All here are much your's. Dear M.[r] Mason,

Your most affectionate

R. HURD

P.S. Remember me to M.[r] Gray, if he be still with you. His british Ode, and the conclusion of his other, are wonderfully admired by D.[r] W.[8]

---

[5] [The allusion is probably to Pitt. In Mason's *Ode* to the younger Pitt (*Works*, I, p. 68) he states in a footnote: the Poem of *Caractacus* was read in MS. by the late Earl of Chatham, who honoured it with an appreciation, which the Author is here proud to record.]

[6] See L. VIII, n. 5.

[7] John Home's *Douglas* was produced in 1756.

[8] [Gray wrote to Thomas Wharton on 7 Oct. 1757: "D.[r] Warburton is come to town, and likes them (the Odes) extremely". Tovey, I, p. 366. See L. XXXVI, n. 2.]

XVII

HURD *to* Mason

Dear Sir,

Prior Park, 21 Dec. 1757

We are perfectly satisfied, or rather delighted, with every part of your and M⸢r⸣ G.'s conduct, with regard to the Lawrell.[1] It could not be for the credit of either of you to accept it. And, to tell you my plain mind, it should not have been offerred. But great men never think greatly. As to W.[2] we hope he will succeed, and are of opinion that the thing is more suitable to his situation and character. He has lost his dignity long since by throwing himself into a dependance, without a Profefsion. Besides you know my opinion (tho' I have the greatest esteem and value for his other virtues) that he has no great poetical dignity to sustain. On the whole, tho' I would not for a Bprick have seen your temples entwined with this tarnishd lawrel, I shall rejoyce to see it flourish on his head. The salary will be a pretty addition to the little things he has got:[3] and

---

[1] On 12 Dec. 1757, Colley Cibber, the poet laureate, died. The Duke of Devonshire, who was Lord Chamberlain, wished the post to be offered to Gray, and his brother, Lord John Cavendish, commissioned Mason (who was then in town) to write to Gray (Mason, *Memoirs*, p. 258). [Gray's letter, in which he declined the offer, is not extant: a later letter of December 19 contains his scornful comment on the office (Tovey, I, p. 372). From Mason's own account it seems unlikely that the post was offered to him. In his Life of Whitehead, which he added to the edition of Whitehead's *Poems* (III, p. 87), he wrote: "I was not myself overlooked on the occasion: so far from it that a previous apology was made to me by Lord John Cavendish, Couched in these or very similar terms, 'that being in orders, I was thought, merely on that account, less eligible for the office than a layman'".]

[2] William Whitehead was made poet laureate on 19 Dec. 1757.

[3] Whitehead was Secretary and Registrar of the Order of the Bath.

'tis bad trusting, in his case, for others of more credit or value. It is entertaining, as you say, the prudery of Garrick. As if one player were not as fit stuff to make a Laureate of, as another.

You will pick up many things, I dare say, for your purpose out of the Druidical books, the Dean sent you.[4] We return to town in January. I believe I must be in Grovnor Square. D.[r] W. is so kind in prefsing me to be with him, and my inclinations, you may be sure, draw so strongly that way, that I shall not go about to excuse myself from giving him that trouble. The dialogues,[5] I believe, will go to the prefs. But to be at leisure to attend to the printing and revision of them, I shall in all likelihood withdraw pretty soon to Cambridge.

The family are much your's. D.[r] W. is always talking to me about Caractacus. The fame of this play, when made into what you will make it, is the only true Lawrel for your wearing.

Believe me, my dear friend,

Your's most inviolably

R. HURD

[4] ["The Druidical books" Mason wanted as authorities for the beliefs of the ancient Britons in his *Caractacus*; the subject is discussed in his correspondence with Gray at this time (see Tovey, II, pp. 5, 12, 16–17). He alludes to two volumes of Pelloutier's *Histoire des Celtes* which Dr Warburton had sent to him.]

[5] [Hurd's *Moral and Political Dialogues* were not published until 1759.]

XVIII

Hurd *to* Mason

My dear Mr Mason,

I thank you for your welcome present of Caractacus. And, formality apart, let me frankly own to you the pride and pleasure I take in seeing myself adorned by you in this fine prelude[1] to the finest of your poems. My vanity is, no doubt, indulged on this occasion; but what makes your partial encomiums truly acceptable to me, is, that I love the person and honour the virtues of the encomiast. This last consideration, I think, more than our kindred studies, has linked our hearts together; a connection, of all others the most firm & indiſsoluble. But enough of this. What the public reception of your work will be I know not. A better age, as you say, must do you justice in that particular.

---

[1] [Mason's *Caractacus* was published on 30 May 1759.] It has prefixed an *Elegy to the Rev. Mr Hurd*, dated 20 March 1759. This was printed as Elegy IV in Mason, *Works* (1811), I, p. 104:

> "Yes, 'tis my pride to own, that taught by thee
>   My conscious soul superior flights essay'd;
> Learnt from thy love the Poet's dignity,
>   And spurn'd the hirelings of the rhyming trade.
>   .   .   .   .
> Whose equal mind could see vain fortune shower
>   Her flimsy favours on the fawning crew,
> While, in low Thurcaston's sequester'd bower,
>   She fix'd him distant from Promotion's view;
> Yet, shelter'd there by calm Contentment's wing,
>   Pleased he could smile, and, with sage HOOKER's eye,
> 'See from his mother earth God's blessings spring,
>   And eat his bread in peace & privacy'".

The reference is to a sentence in a letter from Hooker to Whitgift, quoted in Isaak Walton's *Life* (Hooker, *Works*, Oxford (1875), I, p. 20).

But for the present I must think you have consulted but ill for yourself by sacrificing to friendship, instead of Greatneſs. You have softened very properly one obnoxious paſsage in the elegy, but there are who will not easily forgive so insulting a preference.

I will do as you desire with regard to the omiſsion of the human-sacrifice apology. But to me human sacrifices, and the belief of the Unity are incompatible. I see how difficult it was to make your chorus *favere bonis* in this instance. Yet they might have dropped one word of disapprobation. I doubt our critical friend will not be easily satisfied, especially as I happen'd to say to him the other day that you *had converted the whole play by the hints which he had sent to you by me from P[rior] P[ark]*.[2] This of the sacrifices was what he preſsed most. So that I think you should take some notice of it, when you write to him. You may say that you had designed an alteration (and it may be right to send it him) but that everybody objecting to it as cold & uninteresting in that place, you had left it out. You may further say, as you do to me, that the Chorus give no sanction to human sacrifices,[3] & that the proposal may the rather

[2] This is what Gray described to Mason as the "joint criticism from Prior Park" (Tovey, II, p. 79). He could "recollect what a prejudice the parsons expressed to human sacrifice"; but *Caractacus* "convinced me of the propriety of the thing".
[3] The reference seems to be to *Caractacus* (Mason, *Works* (1811), II, p. 160):

" *Chorus.*

O think not, King,
That Mona shall be curst by these dire rites.
Ev'n from the youth of Time yon holy altar
Has held the place thou seest; ages on ages
Have there done sacrifice; but never yet
Stream'd it with human gore, nor ever shall
While we hold office here".

45

be indulged as suiting the fiercenefs of his character. Something of this sort, at least, I shall say to him. For Caractacus is such a favourite with him that I would not have him indisposed towards it by this omifsion.

I have read the printed sheets once over, and think you have improved many places, especially the part of the chorus towards the conclusion. I shall read it again more critically. The Heb.[4] Society are pleasant people. The truth is, I find myself every day more indifferent to the reputation of a good writer; but I should not enjoy myself in this *sequesterd bower*[5] as I do, if my heart were not attuned to your's in every virtuous affection. My dear Sir, most inviolably

Your obliged friend & Servant

Thurcaston,   R. HURD
1 June, 1759

P.S. Could not you send me *Optime*,[6] & *the Letter from a Blacksmith* under Mr Fraser's covers?[7]

[With this letter is a letter of Thomas Nevile to Hurd of 1 June 1759, expressing his opinion of Mason's play, and a paper headed "General Criticism of Dr Balguy". These were presumably sent by Hurd to Mason.]

[4] [Richard Hurd wrote "Heberden" above the line. The allusion may be to Dr Heberden and his friends in town.]
[5] [Mason's Elegy to Hurd, quoted in n. 1: "in low Thurcaston's sequester'd bower".]
[6] [Hurd probably meant to write *Optimisme*. See L. XIX.]
[7] See L. XXXIV, n. 4.

XIX

HURD *to* Mason

Dear Mr Mason

You don't write, and yet you knew I am quite alone, and you knew too how much I depend on your Letters for the relief of my solitude. I thank you however for sending me the two pamphlets, I spoke of. There is much truth, but no great wit or humour in the Letter from the Blacksmith. If the writer of Douglas be the author,[1] I am much scandalized with the indecency of such a satyr on the establishd church of Scotland, from a member and a minister of it. But this is nothing to the license and effrontery of the other man of wit, who has not learnd that Lesson, which even Dunces ought to learn—*not to scorn his God.* Voltaire is the most infamous writer of his age, and in nothing discovers the littlenefs of his genius more than in writing to the level of the most infamous part of his readers. The *mens divinior* never stoops so low. Even the Atheist Lucretius is always *moral*, which the author of *Candide*[2] is not. Besides Lucretius had a celebrated sect of philosophers on his side, amongst whom were

---

[1] [*A Letter by A. T., Blacksmith, on the public worship of the Church of Scotland* published in 1759 has been doubtfully ascribed to John Home, author of *Douglas.*]

[2] [Voltaire's *Candide ou l'Optimisme* was published in 1758. Warburton did not take so serious a view of it as Hurd. In a postscript to his letter to Hurd of 8 July 1759 (*Letters*, p. 213), he wrote: "The real design of the Candide is to recommend *naturalism*: the professed design is to ridicule the *Optimisme* not of Pope, but of Leibnitz....I find it is understood to be a ridicule on Pope's. But we do not know the figure the *Optimisme* makes in Germany. You will wonder perhaps, the translation was made on my recommendation".]

some of the most virtuous men at Rome. Our poet's sect is only the rabble of corrupt men in shameless courts and debauch'd Cities. And so much for *L'Optimisme*.

Dᴿ Warburton says he has receivd your Letter, and intends to write to you, I believe to scold you for your human Sacrifices. I confefs, I wish this only blemish were remov'd from your tragedy, as I hope it will be in some future edition. Dᴿ Balguy would tell you the fine things our friend says of your Odes. Let me know if so much as one fashionable reader about the court be of the same opinion. The Ladies, I doubt, will give you up as too refin'd and too learned for them.

You talk'd of returning soon to Aston.[3] May I expect the pleasure of seeing you here on your way? I stay here till the end of July, and then remove most probably to Weymouth. Send me a bushell of news about Caractacus, and say for pity if you have found one reasonable creature that speaks well of the Dialogues. I have much to apprehend. For even you are a little squeamish about the Notes, and Millar[4] makes no scruple to condemn the Preface.[5]

People are so silly as to encourage my vanity by writing me compliments, from all quarters, on your Elegy.

[3] [Mason held the living of Aston near Sheffield from 1753 until his death.]

[4] Andrew Millar (1707–68), one of the publishers of Johnson's Dictionary (and of the *Dialogues* above-mentioned).

[5] [The Preface took the form of a pretended dialogue between the Editor and "a bookseller of good repute", in which the number to be printed and likely to be sold is ironically discussed.]

If you did not think to do it, pray send a copy of Caractacus to your great admirer, D.ʳ Macro.⁶

Dear M.ʳ Mason

Your's eternally

Thurcaston   R. HURD

25 June 1759

It must be directed to him at Norton to be left at M.ʳ Lambert's in the Cook-Row, Bury.

XX

HURD *to* Mason

Thurcaston, Nov. 30 1760

Dear Sir,

I have receiv'd your pitiful Letter of the 19ᵗʰ from Cambridge & don't care to tell you, at this moment, what I think of you. Your best way will be to send me your Poem¹ directly. It may be *mactatâ veniam lenior hostiâ.*² Tho' I tell you beforehand, if your poem be not excellent, I am determin'd to dislike it. You think to bespeak my favour by the opinion of M.ʳ Gray.³ As if I car'd for twenty of your own trade. You must turn to your Horace for a proper idea of a Critic,

Impiger, iracundus, inexorabilis, acer.⁴

⁶ See L. IX, n. 1.

¹ [*Elegy on the Death of a Lady* (Lady Coventry): Mason, *Works*, I, p. 107.]

² Horace, *Odes*, I, 19, 16.

³ [Mason had apparently seen Gray in town and had shown him his Elegy. He wrote from Aston on 28 Nov.: "You will find I have altered all the things you marked" (Tovey, I, p. 177). Gray replied on 10 Dec. (*ibid.* p. 178): "It is not good to give copies of a thing before you have given it the last hand" and he submitted the poem to drastic correction. Gray was an inexorable critic.]   ⁴ Horace, *Ars Poetica*, 121.

After all, to show you how well prepar'd I am for a piece of Poetry, I just now come from the reading of Tafso's *Gierusal. Liberata*;[5] in which it is my odd fortune to dislike ev'ry thing which Voltaire, & such critics as He, commend, & to admire evrything which they censure. As a Copyist of Virgil and the antients, He is but feeble, and pafsable at the best. As an original painter of the world of magic & enchantments, he is inimitable. On the whole, no french man is capable of entering into the merits of this extraordinary poem. With all its blemishes it will live when a hundred *Henriades* are justly forgotten.

You don't say a word of new books. Yet somebody spoke to me the other day of a history, by this Voltaire, of *Peter the Great*.[6] His taste for this sort of writing is as singular, as for Epic poetry. He has written, I think, three histories, that of Louis XIV, of Charles the XII, and now of Czar Peter: i.e. of a Swaggerer, a Madman, & a Savage. The only book he ever writ, that reads like a history, & is indeed a fit subject for one, is his Epic Poem.

The Bp, you say, is much pester'd with businefs.[7] I believe, he is; yet I have rarely been a week without receiving a Letter from him. This raises my ideas prodigiously of your late engagements.

---

[5] Hurd had two copies of *Gerusalemme Liberata*; Bernardo Castello's edition, Genova, 1617, 4to; and the Venice folio, 1745, which was given to him in 1804 by Edward Waldron, Rector of Rushock and Headmaster of Hartlebury Grammar School.

[6] [Voltaire's *Histoire de l'Empire de Russie sous Pierre le Grand* was published in 1759.]

[7] Warburton had been consecrated in Lambeth Palace Chapel as Bishop of Gloucester on 20 Jan. 1760. The Bishop of Worcester, James Johnson, assisted.

I desire to be remember'd to M⸍ and M⸍ˢ Wood.[8]
I am more than you deserve.

Your affect. friend & servant
R. HURD

XXI

HURD *to* Mason

My Dear M⸍ Mason

I am not one of those who condole with you on the
resignation of Lord H.[1] Because I think he will be
full as able to serve you now, as when he was in place.
Then the D[uke of] N[ewcastle] disposed of everything.
Now there is a chance at least for this department's
falling into other hands. You see the difference. But
whatever comes of this, you do right to stay in town[2]
for some time, for the reasons you mention. If, after
all, things do not succeed,[3] as your friends wish, by
all means come hither to me. We are made to comfort
each other, or rather we are made to be happy in each
other, with⸍ standing in need of any comfort, under
such petty disappointments as these. Take my word
for it, my dear friend, we are neither of us fated to
be rich.[4]..For I hold we were born under the same
stars, tho' their various influence destined you to be a
great poet, and me to be a poor critic. But, courage,

[8] [John Wood, an undergraduate friend of Mason's at St
John's, was his curate at Aston from 1759 to 1762.]
[1] Lord Holdernesse ceased to hold office as Secretary of State,
12 Mar. 1761.
[2] The letter is addressed to Mason at Lord Holdernesse's house
in Arlington Street.
[3] [The allusion is probably to Mason's hope of a canonry.
See L. XXII, n. 4.]
[4] After this sentence thirteen lines have been erased.

51

my friend. We will be happy in spite of our starrs, I mean your poetry, & my criticism. Heaven has given us an equivalent for this curse, in the blessing of an equal mind. It has done more. It has given us, what no fortune could have done, the love and friendship of each other. I have said all in saying this. Let preferments go which way they will. You and I can do very well in our country parsonages.

> Vive sine invidia; mollesque inglorius annos
> Exige: amicitias et tibi junge pares.[5]
> Dixi.

I charge you, get this Distich engrav'd in Church Letters on yᵉ front of your new building towards the Garden, immediately.—Let Mʳ Wood get it executed agˢᵗ you come home. Mʳ Wood and I for want of better, will stand for the *pares*.[6]

I am not surprized that Mʳ Gray and other fine readers should dislike *Nouvelle Heloise*.[7] I see a hundred reasons for this. The admirers of *Crebillon*[8] are out of their element here. To tell you my opinion in one word this is the most exquisite work of the kind that ever was written. I have read it a second time, & could read it twenty times, with fresh pleasure. The reason is, the author is a man of *virtue*, as well as genius. This *last* indeed is so transcendant in him, that it makes one overlook the most improbable & worst contrived story

---

[5] [Ovid, *Tristia*, III, 4, 143–4.]

[6] [This passage has been written as a postscript in the margin of the letter.]

[7] [Rousseau's *La Nouvelle Héloise* was published in 1760. Gray in a letter to Mason, of 22 Jan. 1761 (Tovey, II, p. 195), had alluded to its "absurdity and insipidity".]

[8] [Gray's fondness for the "romances of Marivaux and Crébillon" is expressed in a letter to West of April 1742 (Tovey, I, p. 97).]

that ever was. But, if he had totally wanted Genius, the magic of his *Virtue* is enough to charm evry reader, who is not wholly devoid of it, himself. The part I like least is the character of Lord Bornston & his Italian amours. But the rocks of Meillery, & the domestic transactions of Clarens are above everything that is extant in the world, of that kind.—The age must be very different from what it is, before such a work as this can be relished at London & Paris. Let them dote on *Crebillon & Voltaire*, as usual: this homely Swifs, for my money. In short, I am of the author's mind: men & women may speak ill of it, and welcome: But let no man or woman speak ill of it to me: I am confident I could never esteem such person, as long as I lived.

It is as violent a transition as any in your Odes to pafs at once from *Roufseau*, to *Stern*.[9] Yet in speaking of Romances, I must tell you my mind of his. The 3^{d} Vol. is insufferably dull and even stupid. The 4th is full as humorous as either of the other two. But this broad humour, even at its best, can never be endured in a work of length. And he does not seem capable of following the advice which one gave him—*of laughing in such a manner, as that Virgins and Priests might laugh with him.*[10]

To return to *Roufseau*, pray read him again and again. You will think evry other Romance-writer (I

---

[9] [The third and fourth volumes of *Tristram Shandy* were published early in 1761. In a letter to Warburton, written on March 18, Hurd had written of *Tristram Shandy* in the terms that he uses here, and also expressed his admiration of Rousseau's work (Warburton, *Letters*, p. 239).]

[10] [A part of the letter, containing three lines of text, has been cut out at this point.]

53

had almost said, not excepting Cervantes himself, but
his manner is too different to be compared with
Roufseau's) poor and contemptible to him. Pick up
what you can in relation to his history, situation, &
private morals. I have an extreme curiosity to be
better acquainted with him. I say, do all this, and let
me see you here as soon as you can. With or without a
Prebend is nothing either to you or me.

> With all affection, my dear Sir,
>
> Most faithfully & for ever
>
> Your's
>
> R. HURD

Thurcaston
30 March 1761

XXII

HURD *to* Mason

Dear Sir

You are an impudent bard, that you are, to satirise
two Lords at once,[1] & certainly fall under the Statute
of *Scandalum Magnatum*, in the proper sense. However

---

[1] [In Mason's MS. *Commonplace Book* there is an "Epigram occasioned by Lord Hardwicke's and Lord Lyttelton's verses to one
another", with a note "Printed in the St James's". In the *St
James's Chronicle* for 25 April 1761 the verses appeared anonymously:

> "While every Freeman in the nation,
> Burgefs and Cit of each Vocation,
>   In PITT's just praises join;
> Thy meagre Virtue, modest Peer!
> Hangs dangling by a single Hair,
>   In H[ardwick]'s hitching Line.
> Indeed, my Lord, you're much to blame
> To risk so rashly your good Name.
>   'Tis true his rhymes are terse;
> Yet honest Folks your Lordship knows,
> So seldom trust a Lawyer's Prose,
>   They'll neer believe his Verse".]

it is my weaknefs to approve all you do. The Epigram is not without its salt. Tho' what you mean by writing such lawlefs things, at the time you are sollicting pre-ferment, I cannot imagine. Learn of Dr Squire[2] or Dr Pyle,[3] to correct your style and manner, or I de-nounce the pains of poverty & poetry upon you, as long as you live.

Your thought of meeting me at P. Park is excellent. The Bp visits sooner than I expected, so that I shall be with him, I hope without fail, before the end of the month. Your being there to receive me, will give me fresh spirits for this long journey. I charge you, don't disappoint me. I shall accept no excuse, unlefs it be the Residentiariship of York.[4]

Your present of the Dialogue[5] was very welcome & unexpected. I had heer'd nothing of it. It shows me, what my vanity would not let me see before, I mean the reason why my Dialogue of famous memory was so ill received by you judges. It was not the *form*, as you flatterers pretended. It was the *execution* that did all the mischief. If I had known how to write like Roufseau, it's succefs had been certain. But to have done with this fond subject, myself, & to say a word

[2] Samuel Squire, Clerk of the Closet, 1756; Dean of Bristol, 1760; Bishop of St Davids, 1761; through obtaining the favour of the Duke of Newcastle and Lord Chesterfield.

[3] [Edmund Pyle, D.D., Archdeacon of York. Both he and Squire were colleagues of Mason's as Court Chaplains.]

[4] [Mason was expecting the reversion of a Residentiary Canonry at York. See his letter to Gray of 20 July 1761 (Tovey, II, p. 219). The vacancy did not occur until January 1762.]

[5] [In February 1761 there was published: "Préface de la Nouvelle Héloise: ou Entretien sur les Romans, entre l'Éditeur et un Homme de Lettres. Par J. J. Rousseau, Citoyen de Genève. Paris, 1761". This was printed as a second preface to later editions of the *Nouvelle Héloise*.]

of *the Citizen of Geneva*. His *entretien* is excellent. Yet how M.ʳ Gray should like it so much, after liking the *Letters* so little, I cannot imagine. It looks as if he began to be ashamed of his former judgment. There is nothing in the Dialogue, but what he had said, or at least intimated up & down in his work. I repeat it, M.ʳ Mason, the man that does not approve the N. Heloise, cannot evidently be approved by me.[6] And I have accordingly required D.ʳ Balguy (who by the way is at Bath, & will be there till towards the end of this month) to retract his opinion of it, on the pain of my utmost displeasure.

I have just finish'd a trifle in 12 short Letters,[7] which you & one or two more will perhaps take the trouble of reading, & which no body else will. I may perhaps take the fancy to bring it with me to Prior-Park.[8]

You are a pitiful philosopher. Talk of pique & I know not what, because great men take no notice of you! Do you know, that if you deserved their countenance & preferments, I should not esteem you half as much as I do? Be content with my esteem, with.ᵗ a prebend. I can tell you, it is not lavished away upon so many, as that it should seem a trifle to you.

I quit this magnificent style to tell you, I expect a Letter from you forthwith, whether you go to Prior-

[6] Gray (Tovey, II, p. 249) wrote: "The *Héloise*...has its Partisans, among wch are Mason and M.ʳ Hurd".

[7] *Letters on Chivalry and Romance*, published in 1762.

[8] Warburton wrote to Hurd, 15 May 1762 (*Letters*, p. 248): "I have now seen the whole of the letters on Chivalry, and am wonderfully taken with them. They should be published forthwith".

Park or no. God blefs you, my dear Sir; Accept this benediction from my Lord Bp of Gloucester's unworthy Chaplain & from

your afsured friend

Thurcaston   R. HURD

May 3 1761

XXIII

HURD *to* Mason

Dear Mʳ Mason   *Thurcaston Oct. 28, 1761*

I had your flying Letter from the North-road, & was much disappointed in your not coming this way, as it was amongst the principal pleasures I had promis'd myself this winter. You may go on with your prefs-work, & send me the sheets when you please.[1] I shall have nothing better to do, than to attend to them.

You hear what a clamour there is about Mʳ Pitt's accepting the King's acknowledgements of his late services. Such a monster, is this many-headed beast. But you, who are not of this spirit,[2] have methinks a fine opportunity to do something in your own way by planning an Ode on this famous Resignation. It would take in all the glories of his ministry: a subject, worthy of your pen, & perhaps the only one of the kind

[1] [Mason's next publication was his *Elegies*, which appeared at the end of 1763. But the reference to his *Odes* in the next letter suggests that he was contemplating the collected edition of his poems, which he published in 1764. See L. XXV, n. 2.]

[2] [Pitt resigned on October 5, 1761, and accepted a pension, with the title of Baroness Chatham for his wife. His admirers, and Mason among them, were distressed. Gray wrote ironically to Brown on October 22 (Tovey, II, p. 241): "We are all much out of countenance about this pension. I . . . expect to hear Mason has taken Laudanum".]

which our times are likely to furnish. There would be a dignity in such a panegyric at this season, & besides it would mortify certain great men. 'Tis true, of the prudence of this project I can say nothing.

I have just been reading *Crevier's history of the University of Paris*.[3] I can by no means recommend it to you. What would you think of a history, in form, of our famous University of Cambridge? And yet our never to be forgotten squabbles about Appeals[4] would make as shining a chapter, as any you will find in these labour'd volumes. I sent for them on the supposition of their being a *literary* history. Alaſs! they are only an *Academical*.

But I have a higher entertainment than this in view. To say nothing of Hume's abridged English history[5] from Julius Caesar to Henry VII (just now publish'd) w^ch, I suppose like his other things will be just worth the reading, I have got the best Paris edition of Plutarch's works,[6] & these I depend upon for my winter's amusement.

In fact, anything is better than turning ones thoughts on the men & things of these times. Yet I shall always be attentive to anything in which you are interested. Let me hear a word of your Stall at York; or at least that you are well & easy out of it. Dear Mr Mason, your most affectionate friend & Servt

R. HURD

  [3] [*L'Histoire de l'Université de Paris depuis son origine jusqu'en l'année* 1600, by J. B. L. Crevier, was published in 1760.]
  [4] [See L. V, n. 2.]
  [5] [Hume's previously published volumes had covered the history from Henry VIII to James II. In 1761 two volumes on the history down to Henry VII appeared.]
  [6] His library contains *Plutarchi Opera*, the eight volume folio edition, Lutetiae Parisiorum, 1624.

XXIV

Hurd *to* Mason

Thurcaston 27 Nov. 1761

Dear M͏ͬ Mason

Tho' you affirm roundly, you are quite mistaken, at least in this instance, in thinking that my opinion of M͏ͬ P[itt] was determin'd by that of our friend.[1] I did not at that time so much as know what was his opinion. I consider'd the case in this view. A pension & peerage were, I own, suspicious circumstances. But when I understood that these were not bargain'd for, nor so much as ask'd, it seem'd to me that they could not be refus'd without indecency, without reflecting upon the K..., nor indeed without an evident degree of faction. It is very true, & M͏ͬ P. could not but be aware of it, his popularity was likely to suffer by his acceptance of these favours. But this I make a fresh argument for M͏ͬ P.'s honesty, who sacrific'd what was most dear to him, to his loyalty & his Duty. I could say much more, but am contented to rest the matter upon his future conduct, if his past do not satisfy you. In the mean time forgive me this candour: I may not, perhaps, offend in the same sort again very speedily.

Hume's history is entertaining. He says a great deal, & very pertinently, on the feudal System; but nothing that contradicts me,[2] tho' he may possibly be of that opinion. What I did not expect, is, that I receive no new light from him upon this subject. Now this work is completed, I will tell you my sentiments of it in few

[1] Bp Warburton [H].
[2] I.e. in the *Letters on Chivalry and Romance*.

59

words. His *Libertinism* on many occasions is *detestable*: his bigottry to the Stuart family, which occasion'd his political follies, *pernicious*, & his bias to the french taste and manners, which appears thro'out his work, *ridiculous*. Otherwise, this is the most readible General history we have of England. The faults of his *Composition* are, a too frequent affectation of philosophical disquisition; & an incorrect, & sometimes an inflated style. The *former* is unsuited to the general nature of history: And the *latter* is a capital blemish in a work that pretends to be nothing more than a compilation. With these defects, his work will be read & admird: and what is still worse, the mediocrity of this history will prevent an able writer from undertaking a better. DIXI.

As to your Odes,[3] print what you will, provided it be excellent in its kind. I like the *Water-nymph*[4] as much as you do:—I am not for a good writer's condescending —& that is my answer to Mainwaring's sophistical letter.[5]

You grow horridly misanthropical: witneſs your Satires & Comedies. I shall print my innocent Letters on Chivalry forthwith, where there is not a word of ill nature.

Plutarch sends his Love to you, and deserves, I think, to be of your acquaintance. Remember me to your Neighbours at the Parsonage, and believe me very much your's

R. HURD

[3] [See L. XXIII, n. 1.]
[4] [*Ode to a Water Nymph*, written in 1747, and published in Dodsley's *Collection of Poems*, vol. III, and in a revised form later. Mason, *Works*, I, p. 23.]   [5] [Two lines are here erased.]

XXV

HURD *to* Mason

Dear M.ʳ Mason,

You did well to begin your last Letter with so many handsome things on the new Dialogues,[1] or I had shewn no mercy to the concluding part of it, in which you tell me of your design of running away to London. You a Philosopher, indeed! and after your Vignette[2] & *vitam quæ faciunt beatiorem*!—For shame, turn to your Epictetus[3] & learn the difference between τὰ ἐφ' ἡμῖν, and τὰ οὐκ ἐφ' ἡμῖν.—But I have told the Bishop of you & so leave you to his correction.

I have received your very elegant volume, which now flames in the forehead of my Library. When I have your other copy, I shall read you, for the last time, with the severity of a critic. But I believe you are now so polished, that I shall find little to object to you. In the mean time let me thank you for this agreable present. How proud I am of the conspicuous figure[4] I make in it, you will understand from these lines of Ovid, which I have transcribed into the first page.[5]

---

[1] *On the Uses of Foreign Travel*, published in 1763.

[2] [The first collected edition of Mason's *Poems* was published at the end of 1763 (the imprint has the date 1764). The "Vignette" on the title-page is engraved by Basire. It contains emblems of Mason's various pursuits—poetry, painting, music, gardening, bee-keeping, etc.—with the motto (from Martial, x, 47, 1): "vitam quæ faciunt beatiorem".] [3] *Enchiridion*, 1.

[4] [*Elegy III* is addressed *To the Rev. M.ʳ Hurd*, with a note: "this Elegy was prefixt to the former editions of *Caractacus* as dedicatory of that poem". See L. XVIII, n. 1.]

[5] The Bishop's copy (now C. f. 10 in the Hartlebury Library) is inscribed: "The author's present to R. Hurd", with the Ovidian couplet underneath. Ovid, *Amores*, I, 3, 25–6.

Nos quoque per totum pariter cantabimur orbem:
Junctaque erunt pariter nomina nostra Tuis.

I should tell you that my favourite Vignette has not suffered in the least, from binding. The Sonnet[6] is pretty: but you Poets have not a word of truth in you. So well did Fontaine observe of you, in all respects—*Le mensonge et les vers de tout tems sont amis.*

M.ͬ Nevile, not knowing where you are, desires me to convey his thanks for your present to him. The substance of what he says is this—that he approves your omifsions in this volume, but that the exclusion of the Installation Ode[7] will certainly give offence—[This you will not be sorry for]—that the improvements of the *Water-Nymph* are excellent, & that the close of it has now a dignity becoming the author—that, in short, he is much pleased with the whole, which he thinks you have polished very highly, & that the *motto* to Musæus[8] is singularly happy.—As you compliment *my* skill in these things, I will give you the satisfaction to understand, that I am as much pleased with it, as he is.

But now to return, as is natural, to myself. I am much flattered, that the Dialogues are to your taste.

[6] [A Sonnet, dated 12 May 1763, is addressed, as is the Dedication, to the Earl of Holdernesse.]

[7] [The *Ode for Music* written for the Installation of the Duke of Newcastle as Chancellor of the University of Cambridge was not included in Mason's *Collected Works* until the edition of 1797. See *Works*, I, p. 33 n.]

[8] [The motto from Dionysius of Halicarnassus (*De Dinarcho* 7), which Mason added, is as follows: πᾶσι μὲν τοῖς ἀρχετύποις αὐτοφυής τις ἐπιπρέπει χάρις, καὶ ὥρα. τοῖς δ' ἀπὸ τούτων κατεσκευασμένοις, κἂν ἐπ' ἄκρον μιμήσεως ἔλθωσι, πρόσεστί τι ὅμως τὸ ἐπιτετηδευμένον, καὶ οὐκ ἐκ φύσεως ὕπαρχον.]

As to the *Prediction*,[9] I think a good part of it is, or at least has been fullfilled: & for what remains, the Universities, if they are wise, will understand it as a hint for their further improvement. You may be right in what you say of the court & town Readers. But no management, I suspect, would reconcile them to the subject.

What you mentioned of the Pastorel in Huetius[10] book *de l'esprit*, occasioned me to send for it. It is a detestable one: in short, a system of the grofsest sort of Epicureanism. Besides his libertinism & infidelity, both which are in the extreme, the author is a most egregious coxcomb: but so indeed are all the foreign fashionable philosophers of the time, that I have seen, the *Diderots*, the *D'alemberts*, the *Duclos*, & the rest of them. This modest *Huetius* thinks the science of morals is yet in it's infancy; & I shall think so too, if the world be such a child as to put itself to school to this Philosopher. Now I know the character of the man, I really believe he took his Pastoral poem,[11] *himself*, out of your works, & was coxcomb enough to pafs the plagiarism upon some other. At all events, his testimony can do you no honour. As a *Philosopher*, he is an Adorer of David Hume; and indeed just such another *critic*.

[9] Dialogue viii (Hurd, *Works* (1811), IV, pp. 135 ff.) closes with a fine prophecy by Locke of "the happier scene which a little time shall disclose to your view, in our *English* Universities" (p. 226).

[10] [Huetius appears to be Hurd's slip for Helvetius, whose book *De l'Esprit* was published in 1758.]

[11] [Helvetius in the third chapter of his third Essay professed to give the translation of a piece of English poetry, which Mason recognised as made up of passages from his *Elfrida*. The source was not acknowledged, and Mason in a long note in the *Memoirs* (pp. 296 ff.) discusses "this odd instance of plagiarism".]

Jan. 29. Thus far I had written several days ago, &
then bethought myself that I knew not whither to
direct to you, & so stopped my hand, till I should receive another Letter from you. This I have just now
done, & will therefore resume my pen, tho' I have
already scribbled a reasonable quantity to you. You
flatter me not a little in what you say of M.͟r Gray's
approbation of the Dialogues. Now you & he are of
the same mind, I will presume to think they are not
altogether without merit. There are but two or three
men, whose opinion you & I are sollicitous about.

The world, beside, may censure or commend.[12]

I confefs if M.͟r Gray & you had not been favourable to
those pages you mention, I would never have set pen
to paper again. When I showed the Bp. of Gl. the MS
he singled them out, as you have done. I mention this
to show you how completely my vanity is now satisfied.

But enough, or more than enough, on this subject.
As to your own Book, you certainly mistake the matter.
As there is not much new in it, it might not be much
talked of at present, but every body will purchase it.

I received a Letter from the Profefsor of Poetry[13] at
Oxford, in which are these words—"My most sincere
thanks are due to M.͟r Mason for his kind exprefsions
concerning me. I think he is perfectly right with regard
to his Isis.[14] I hope for the pleasure of seeing many

[12] [Pope, *Imitations of Horace*, Satire 1 of Book 11, l. 122.]
[13] Thomas Warton, Professor of Poetry, 1757–67. Hurd called
him "Honest Tom" (Kilvert, p. 119). [Nine of his letters to
Hurd are preserved at Hartlebury.]
[14] [*Isis*, written by Mason in 1748 and published in 1749, was
an attack on the Jacobite principles prevalent in Oxford. It
provoked Warton to reply in the *Triumph of Isis*. In the edition

64

new things in his Volume". Mr Profeſsor, you see, is short & laconic, & by no means ceremonious; but I believe he means very honestly.

I return to your Letter from Pembroke Hall, I have not seen, & never desire to see the Duellist.[15] Such a wretch is employed, as one would expect, in abusing the Bp & you. But the compliment is half-spoiled, when the honour of his abuse falls upon such as those two others. I think of these two, I believe, just as you do; but depend upon it our Satirist sees no difference. I gueſs at your B.[16] who is said to have commended *the three Characters*,[17] & I love the honest indignation you expreſs upon it.

A propos to our Bishop, you will see him in Town with Mrs Warburton. By the way, he tells me a fine story about you, nothing leſs than that you are going to be married.[18] Was this fair, not to give me one hint of it? He even quotes, for his authority, your friend Lord Delaware,[19] who told him, he believed it was true, but pretended to know nothing of the Party. He

of his poems published in 1763 Mason did not include his *Isis* and Hurd had informed Warton of the intended omission. It was first reprinted in the edition of Mason's *Poems* published in 1797. See *Works*, I, p. 179.]

[15] [Soon after Wilkes had been wounded in a duel by Samuel Martin in November 1763, Churchill published *The Duellist*, in which he bitterly attacked Warburton.]

[16] [Richard Hurd notes "Archbishop Drummond".]

[17] [Warburton, Mansfield and Sandwich, the chief assailants of Wilkes in the House of Lords, are severally denounced in the poem.]

[18] [Gray wrote from Cambridge on February 21, 1764: "Mason has pass'd three weeks with me in his way to Town. The general report was that he was going to be married out of hand: but I find it was only a faint sort of tendency that way" (Tovey, III, p. 32). Mason was not married until September 1765.]

[19] John West, seventh Baron, first Earl De La Warr (1693–1766).

then concludes in these words, so exprefsive of himself —*Whatever there is in it, I wish him happy with all that warmth I bear to my friends: for a worthier man lives not.* I mention this to shew you that the warmth, you exprefsed on the occasion mentioned above, is not likely to be thrown away (as the warmth of friendship too often is) on a man insensible, or unworthy of it.—But as to this *marriage*, it runs strangely in my head. I am the more inclined to believe, there may be something in it, as I remember you did not tast my raillery at Aston, when, for want of other subjects to divert our *ennui*, it would sometimes fall on that topic. See that you tell me the whole truth, & speedily too. You may safely do it, for, notwithstanding the liberties I may sometimes take, as a Batcheler & Badineer, yet, as Milton says[20] *I deem mysteriously of the genial Bed*, & no doubt think with Solomon (tho' it be a Text indeed I never preach upon) that *He who findeth a wife findeth a good thing*, as you may read at large in the 18th Ch. of Proverbs & the 22d verse. 'Tis true, that great Clerk, Mr Doctor Kennicot says the text is mutilated, and that it should be (as he pretends to find, it is in some Manuscripts), He that findeth a *good* wife, findeth a good thing. And this way indeed, the afsertion of the wise man is more incontrovertible. But then whether a wise man would deliver so trifling a proposition, as this, that *a good thing is a good thing*, I leave the learned to consider. It is enough that I take the

[20] [Hurd probably had in mind the lines in *Paradise Lost*, viii, ll. 598–9:

Though higher of the genial bed by far,
And with mysterious reverence I deem.]

66

proposition to be true, in a *reasonable* sense, without his emendation. Upon this occasion I have examined your Vignette again, & there I find the *Bust* has a further meaning than I was aware of. It certainly stands for a *Wife*,[21] as one of those good things, *vitam quæ faciunt beatiorem.*

I must still turn another page, but it shall be the last, for the present. God knows when I shall be in town, or whether I shall be there this Spring at all. The Bp. invites me very kindly to Grov'ner Square: & I should rejoyce to bring you back with me. But then this marriage spoils all again. In short, I will not tell you what I shall do, till I heer further from you. In the mean time as you are in a Lord's house, and will see *my* Lord,[22] remember to send me half a dozen franks, of one of their names, for this late Printing has quite ruined me. And if it had not been for your directing me to write under cover to Lord Delaware, there is no knowing what all this paper would have cost you. Yet if I had taken as much more it would but very imperfectly have told you the affection with which I am ever, my Dear Sir, married or unmarried, bond or free,

Your's unalterably
R. HURD

Signed & sealed this 29th of Jan. 1764, but it may be some days, before I have an opportunity of sending to the Post at Leicester.

[21] [The bust manifestly stands for Apollo, but it gives an opportunity for Hurd's badinage.]
[22] [Bishop Warburton.]

XXVI

Hurd *to* Gray

Dear Sir,

I troubled you some time ago, by Mr Mason, with a petition in behalf of Mr T. Warton,[1] who is digesting his history of E. Poetry, & wishes very much to know what your idea was for the scheme of such a work. I told him, I did not know what progreſs you had made in that design, or whether you had drawn out a plan of it, but that, if you had, I believed you would readily acquaint him with it.[2] This paſſed in the Summer, & since that I have heard nothing of him. But as I suppose you are now in college,[3] after your various wanderings by sea & land,[4] you will give me a pleasure to let me know what I shall further say on this subject to Mr Warton. If you have any papers to com-

[1] On 26 July 1769 Thomas Warton wrote to Hurd reminding him of his offer made during a visit to Oxford "to ask Mr Gray for the Plan he had formed of the *History of English Poetry*". He had gone into the country to collect his materials and "finish a work to which my Studies have long been directed, under your kind encouragement and the flattering hopes of your Approbation". See L. XIV, n. 5.

[2] [On 15 April 1770 Gray wrote to Warton, excusing his delay in complying with the request communicated to him by Dr Hurd and sending "a sketch of the division or arrangement of the subject". See Tovey, III, pp. 276 ff.] In Warton's Preface to the first volume of his *History of English Poetry* (1774), he explains the relation of Gray's plans to "Mr Pope's scheme" of which Mason "a few years ago" with "that liberality which ever accompanies true genius" had given him an authentic copy.

[3] The letter is inscribed: "To Thomas Gray Esqr at Pembroke Hall, Cambridge" but was re-addressed: "Mr Roberts's Hosier and Hatter, at the three Squirrels in Jermyn Street, London".

[4] [In this year Gray was away from Cambridge from early in July until nearly the end of October, and in the latter month made a tour of the Lakes.]

municate to him, & will send them to me, I will take care they shall be transmitted safely to Oxford. I believe I may answer to you for him, that he will make no improper use of your favours.

Of Mr Mason I hear nothing, except, by D.̣ Gisburne,[5] that he is now at Aston. He complains, that you and I are hyper-critical, or rather hyper-political: But in this he is mistaken: We only wish to see his Georgic,[6] truly Virgilian.

M.̣ Nevile has sent me his *Imitations*.[7] They are not to be considered, as *Satires*, for popular reading; but as *clafsical amusements*, sometimes copying the sense, & sometimes the manner, of his originals. And in this light, they have frequently great merit.

You did not send me a copy of the Installation Ode;[8] which piqued me, so much, that I was greatly disappointed when, with so good a disposition to find fault, I was obliged, with all the world, to commend & admire it.

> I am very truly, Dear Sir,
>
> Your affectionate humble
>
> Servant
>
> R. HURD

Lincoln's Inn, Dec. 4, 1769

[5] [Thomas Gisborne, M.D., Fellow of St John's College, Cambridge, a friend of Gray and Mason, was a physician in London.]
[6] *The English Garden.*
[7] [Thomas Nevile (L. II, n. 5) in 1769 published *Imitations of Juvenal and Persius.*]
[8] *Ode performed in the Senate-House at Cambridge, July 1, 1769, at the Installation of his Grace Augustus Henry Fitzroy, Duke of Grafton, Chancellor of the University.*

XXVII

HURD *to* Mason

Lincoln's Inn, Jan. 22, 1770

Dear Sir,

You are very good to inquire after my health, wch has not been what I could wish, yet not so bad as you had heered. I am still under Dr Heberden's direction, & my prospects are not the most encouraging. But *fiat voluntas tua* is, you know, at once our duty, & our consolation.

You do well to build a house for your Succefsor, who may be in no condition to build one for himself. I suspect, however, that you may be weary of Aston, before the winter is over; And yet I know not how to invite you into this turbid & distracted scene. I think it is your own fault to be so much taken up with people, you do not care for, when you are in town. I live here more to myself than anywhere else; & my only secret is, that I do not encourage idle people to come about me, because I can amuse myself without their company. Why cannot you do the same, you, who have more sources of amusement, than I have? And then we might see each other often, & not be at the mercy of those who have nothing but their own vanity to indulge, in breaking in upon us. If you come hither with this resolution, I shall be heartily glad to see you, because your coming will contribute very much to my happinefs. But if you are to waste your time upon other people, my selfishnefs makes me think you may as well be where you are. Yet if it be but for the chance of getting you by my fire-side now & then, I cannot wholly discourage your taking a journey to this place.

I confefs you are as good & obedient a subject, as any critic could wish. Yet I am by no means ag^st your resuming the project of your poem.[1] There are many fine things in it, &, with a little trouble, the whole would be to my mind. But more of this, when I see you. Mr Nevile's publication,[2] tho' not entirely with, was not altogether against, my consent. He found these things amusing to him, & they are not without merit. But his whole design is now finished: & what I chiefly recommend to him, is the revisal of his Georgics.[3] I am not fond of translations, but this, with some care, will be excellent, & is, at present, far better than any other we have of that exquisite work.

The events of this last week have been various & interesting. The removal of one Chancellor,[4] & the choice of another, & the death of this last,[5] agitate the minds of men differently, as their sentiments & passions happen to be engaged. For myself, I have lost a friend, in Mr Y. I knew he had his foibles, but he was a virtuous & amiable man. I wish the public may not have reason to regret his lofs.

[1] [*The English Garden.* See L. XXVI, n. 6.]
[2] [See L. XXVI, n. 7.]
[3] [In 1767 Nevile published a *Translation of the Georgics of Virgil.*]
[4] Charles Pratt, first Baron (afterwards Earl) Camden, was Lord Chancellor in Chatham's Ministry of 1768, but was deprived of the office, Jan. 1770, through his disagreement with the American policy.
[5] Charles Yorke, son of Philip, first Earl of Hardwicke, Lord Chancellor, was appointed to succeed Camden as Lord Chancellor, Jan. 1770, but died suddenly and mysteriously within a few hours.

71

You apprehend *my labour in lecturing* to be greater, than it really is. Not but I have taken some trouble to satisfy others, and still more myself. To set your honest heart at ease, this trouble is now over, at least for the present. I yesterday preached my *fifth* lecture[6] on Prophecy & have completed the rough draft of the XII. What remains is only to correct & polish, which I consider as an amusement, rather than a Labour. If you ask me, how I am satisfied with the whole, now it lies before me, I answer, tolerably. Mʳ Gray thinks, and perhaps with reason, that I shall not convince others.[7] What is more important, I have convinced myself; or, to expreſs myself more properly, the result of my speculations has been to strengthen the conviction, I before had. I thought the argument from prophecy had real weight, or I could not have written upon it: I now think it momentous in the highest degree. I understand more than I did, & I adore what I do not yet fully comprehend. If men could be brought to do the last (which surely is not unreasonable, when the subject is so sublime), they would be content to read their Bible, & not to write against it. When I consider things in a certain light, I know not whether I should more pity, or despise, such precious scribblers as Voltaire & D'Alembert.

[6] The fifth of Hurd's Warburtonian lectures dealt with "Prophecies concerning Christ's First Coming". The series was published in the spring of 1772, with a dedication to the surviving trustees, Lord Mansfield and Sir John Eardley Wilmot, and with a note lamenting the sudden death of the third, the Hon. Charles Yorke. *Luctuosum hoc suis; acerbum patriae; grave bonis omnibus.* Cic. [*De oratore*, III, 2, 8].

[7] Warburton's view was characteristic: "I am glad you have dispatched the fourth sermon. The more they have of you, the better for them" (*Letters*, p. 335; 7 Dec. 1769).

The Bishop & Mrs W. are here, & frequently ask after you. They are both well, &, I think, likely to spend a good deal of their time in London. With this view, as I conclude, they have made many & great improvements in their House in G. Square.

My paper is so nearly run out, that I have only room to wish you all happinefs this new year & to tell you that every revolving year, as it comes about, but adds to the sincere affection, with which I am ever,

Dear Sir,

Your's

R. HURD

P.S. The *trip to Scotland*[8] is Whitehead's. I have not seen it. But they say it is well received.

XXVIII

HURD *to* Mason

Lincoln's Inn, May 8, 1770

Dear Mr Mason

Your long Letter of the 9th past was very kind. When it came I was out of town, & did not return till the end of Easter week; so that you could not receive my Lectures by Lord H[oldernesse]. But, to be honest with you, if I had been at home, I should not have sent them: for I have only one copy, that is fit for use, & I am every day adding or altering something, as fresh hints occur to me.

I know not what to say to Bridlington. It is a long way off; yet, if I proposed amusement to my self in

---

[8] [*The Trip to Scotland*, a farcical play by Whitehead, was produced at Drury Lane on 6 Jan. 1770.]

visiting the Ocean, I should prefer that place to any other for the chance of your company. The truth is, I expect to be out of humour all the time, & out of health too; & it would be a bad compliment to you to make you partake, or even to be a witnefs, of my infirmities. The Bp's visitation will not be over till towards the end of June; & then, & not till then, I shall take my resolution. In the mean time, let me be acquainted with your Motions, that I may suit my self to your convenience, if at length I should resolve for Bridlington.

And why may not I be permitted to see your Argentile?[1] Do you think that I should apply my rules to what is profefsedly written without, & against Rule? That would be, as the comic poet says, *insanire cum ratione*.[2] The case was different with your Georgic:[3] And when you write by rule, I shall never suffer you to swerve an inch from it. After all I am confident, I should like your Argentile; &, at a proper time, I must & will see it.

The amount of my Prophecy was only this, That the faction have mifsed their aim, for the present:[4] what may come hereafter, I know not; or rather *I do know*, for I well remember that, tho' the Catalinarian con-

---

[1] *Argentile and Curan* (Mason, *Works*, II, pp. 207 ff.) is there described as "a legendary drama... written on the Old English Model about the year 1766". It is partly in verse, partly in prose, and was not published till 1797.
[2] [Terence, *Eunuchus*, I, 1, 18.]
[3] *The English Garden*, of which the first book appeared in 1772; and of whose preparation Hurd can now speak in the past tense.
[4] [Walpole (*Letters*, VII, p. 378), writing to Sir Horace Mann on May 6, 1770, alludes to Wilkes: "In truth, his party is crumbled away strangely.... In Parliament their numbers are shrunk to nothing, and the session is ending very triumphantly for the court".]

spiracy was supprefsed, other Catalines sprung up, & Rome expired in no long time after. By the way, I recommend it to you (when you have finished Mosheim, wch is a good book) to read Sallust with care, & then to tell me honestly what you think of our present patriots, & of their virtuous projects in favour of English Liberty. The use of history is only to amuse a few idle men. It never did any other good; because, when the time comes to profit by it, men are too vicious to take the benefit of its instructions. I could moralise in this way thro' the rest of my paper, but think you do well to turn yourself to your Back Gammon, rather than to Politics. I wish you a pleasant game with your Curate, & am ever, my dear Sir, most entirely

Your's

R. H.

XXIX

Hurd *to* Mason

Thurcaston, Oct. 26, 1770

Dear Mr Mason

At length I have your gracious Epistle of the 13th. You do well to scold first, for, if you had not prevented me, *I had prepared me many a stern rebuke*, for your neglect of my last Letter. 'Tis true, I had taken my resolution not to go to Sea, & Dr Heberden acquiesced in it. But I came hither in the beginning of July, & had determined to pafs on to Aston, if I had received notice of your being there, & of your having no company. See what *you* have lost (I do not say, I) by your *nonchalance*, or forgetfulness of me. Here I have been ever

75

since, in no good humour with you, nor always with myself, yet as cheerful as I could, &, when I was tolerably well, not unhappy.

You will ask what I have done in this long leisure. Not much indeed, to any purpose. My Lecture[1] has slept: But I found an amusement in turning over the works of Mr Addison. I set out, many years ago, with a warm admiration of this amiable writer. I then took a surfeit of his natural, easy manner; and was taken, like my betters, with the raptures and high flights of Shakespeare. My maturer judgment, or lenient age (call it which you will) has now lead me back to the favourite of my youth. And here, I think, I shall stick: for such useful sense, in so charming words, I find not elsewhere. His tast is so pure, and his *Virgilian prose* (as Dr Young[2] styles it) so exquisite, that I have but now found out, at the close of a critical life, the full value of his writings.[3]

You make me happy in saying you intend to spend your winter in London. I know you will get as far from me as pofsible. Yet let us come together sometimes, and renew the image, at least, of those enchanting days (enchanting to me, at least) which rolled over us at Cambridge.[4]

You expect *good* to be educed from the *evil* of political opposition. You do well and piously: but do

---

[1] He was still at his Warburtonian Lectures.
[2] [Edward Young (author of *Night Thoughts*) published anonymously in 1759 *Conjectures on Original Composition*. On p. 98 he wrote: "Addison wrote little in Verse, much in sweet, elegant Virgilian Prose".]
[3] [Hurd left material for an annotated edition of Addison which was published in 1811 in six volumes.]
[4] [A paragraph of six lines has here been erased.]

not expect any good from it to our degenerate country. Nor let the cry of *Liberty* mislead you. That cry was as loud, & just as honest, when the divine Cicero put two or three miscreants to death, as it has been with us for the Goodmans fields Maſsacre and the Middlesex Election.

Your Yorkshire patriots may pride themselves on this precedent, for the mighty Julius was the mouth of that patriot company.

As I hope to see you so soon, I meant to say but one word, when I began, & yet have scribbled out my paper. I go to town next week, if these rains will permit, & shall then expect you with impatience.

With all affection, my dear Sir,

Your constant friend & Servant
R. HURD

XXX

HURD *to* Mason

Thurcaston Septr 15, 1771

Dear Mr Mason

Your kind Letter of the 11th found me at this place, where, except for about a fortnight, in which I made an excursion to Birmingham[1] & Gloucester,[2] I have constantly been, since I left London in the end of June.

I shall waste none of my paper in stating the punctilios of our correspondence. Our friendship is above

---

[1] [Hurd's younger brother, Thomas, lived at Birmingham. See Hurd's letter to Warburton, 2 July 1754, *Letters*, p. 117: "We are three brothers of us, . . . the youngest in the Birmingham trade".]

[2] He had been Archdeacon of Gloucester since August 1767.

& beyond every thing of that sort. Poor M.ʳ Gray![3]
I sympathise tenderly with you for the loss of him.[4]
He had many & great virtues, the lustre of which was
a little obscured to those, who did not know him well,
by some peculiarities in his manner, & of which he had
not the full enjoyment himself, from a too splenetic
habit. His learning was considerable; and his taste &
genius above all praise. He showed the sincerity of his
friendship, & at the same time a true judgment, in
leaving his papers to your care. I question not but
many of the *fragments*, you mention, will deserve to be
made public; tho' hardly anything, he could have
finished himself for the prefs, would add much to his
fame, which already is as high, as it well can be, &
yet not higher than is right: So just has this capricious
world been, in one instance, to superior merit! Of his
other MSS there may be room for more deliberation:
And you do well to propose taking the opinion of your
more judicious friends. If you honour me with a place
in this list, you may depend on knowing my real sentiments, whatever they may be.

To return now to the rest of your Letter, in which
you ask kindly after my health, & a little *enviously*, I
think, after my Post-chaise. Of the *first*, let it be
enough to say, that it is better than it has been: And
of the *Second*, that the Coachmaker disappointed me,
at least for this summer, tho' he promises fair against
the next. Most probably I shall trust to him no longer

[3] Gray died on 30 July 1771. Mason was one of his executors,
and had the disposal of his papers.
[4] Two days earlier Hurd wrote (13 Sept. 1771) to Balguy,
describing how Gray had called upon him before Hurd left
London in June; Kilvert, p. 110.

than till I return to town: If I do not find a right good secondhand chaise provided for me by that time, I shall hardly wait any longer, but be impatient & extravagant enough to order a new one to my mind. Will you accept this disappointment, now, as an apology for my not coming to York? To be honest with you, I do not expect that you should. But my little, or great affairs, call them which you will, confine me here for the small remainder of the vacation, which yet, without intending you a compliment, I should spend much more pleasantly with the Præcentor of York.

Poor Balguy has been ill, & much distrefsed in his family connections. Our good Bishop is alone at Gloucester, & deserves a long Letter from you, while Mrs W. is traversing the Emperor's dominions, in company with Mr & Mrs Poultney. This, I think, is all the news I have to tell you, except that my Lord of Lincoln[5] preached a most excellent sermon on Wednesday last at the opening of our Leicester-Infirmary, &, what you will like to hear better, is removing in all hast to Amen-Corner,[6] where you & I shall meet many a good time, it is to be hoped, next winter, as we used to do in Scotland Yard.

Adieu, my dear friend, & believe me,
most unfeignedly your's

R. HURD

[5] John Green. For an amusing light on Hurd's former intimacy with "the Master of Benet", see Kilvert, p. 51.

[6] Green was admitted on 1 Aug. 1771 to the first residentiary canonry of St Paul's, on the ground that the See of Lincoln was ill-endowed.

XXXI

HURD *to* Mason

Lincoln's Inn Decr 24, 1772

And so you expected my compliments on the succeſs of Elfrida, & the honour of your new connection with the Manager of Covent Garden Theatre.[1] To tell you the truth, in one word, I know nothing of plays or players. Not but, as Socrates went to see Euripides' tragedies, it might not have been beneath the dignity of my wisdom to show the same respect to your Elfrida, if constant ill health, wch has attended me ever since I came hither in the end of October, had not kept me at home. All I know is that last night should have been the 18th time of exhibition, if Miss Catley had not been ill....Yes, I can say one thing more: your good friend Ld Mansfield took the French Embaſsador to see Elfrida. The report is said to be favourable enough: Only Orgar's character was thought extravagant. I am told indeed (& so I said in answer to this criticism) that Orgar's part is overacted. In general, they say the action is but indifferent. So that the succeſs, after all, may be owing very much to the Musick, & especially to the *person* of Elfrida. But enough of this.

Dr Balguy's charge is, as you say, an excellent one, and deserves your thanks.[2] It is strange your

[1] *Elfrida* was produced at Covent Garden, 21 Nov. 1772, by Colman, without Mason's knowledge, Dr Arne supplying the music. [See Mason's letter to Walpole of Dec. 1 (*Walpole-Mason Correspondence*, I, p. 45).]

[2] On Subscription to Articles of Religion. Hurd told Balguy that "it will do much good at this juncture" (Kilvert, p. 112).

A.B.³ did not see, that the principles, the author goes upon, are the very reverse of those, wch a certain bench espoused on a late occasion. I think it was but charity for once to set the public right. I suppose, you will hear nothing farther from the author on this subject. He comes to town next week for the winter. Dr Powell's charge is a good one in its way, but on another subject. As to your friend of Lincoln's Inn, set yourself at ease: You will not find him in the hast, again, in the catalogue of authors.

The Mr Wollaston,⁴ you speak of, is brother to my Afsistant—a well-intentioned but weak man. His scheme cannot take. I hear of no body that comes into it, but the Dean of Lincoln, the Master of the Charter-house, and Dr Porteus.⁵

I agree with you: the Bp. of L[incoln] has done

It is Charge No. V in Thos. Balguy, *Discourses on Various Subjects*, Winchester, 1785; Hurd's copy was "from the Author". The charge dealt with the situation created by the Feathers Tavern petition to Parliament in 1772 for the abolition of subscription and for the substitution of a simple profession of belief in Scripture. Balguy posed the question "Whether it be fit for Government to employ and reward equally the Ministers of *all* religions; or to support *one* religion only, and tolerate the rest", adding that "An Establishment without a Toleration is *unjust*: a Toleration without an Establishment is *unintelligible*" (p. 254).

³ Robert Hay Drummond, Archbishop of York, 1761–76.

⁴ [Francis Wollaston, Rector of Chislehurst, published in 1772 *An Address to the Clergy of the Church of England in particular, and to all Christians in general*, in which he supported the proposal to relieve the Clergy and the students of the Universities from the necessity of subscribing to the Thirty-nine Articles. See also n. 5.]

⁵ Porteus' account (R. Hodgson, *Life of Beilby Porteus*, 1812, p. 38) runs thus: "At the close of the year 1772, and the beginning of the next, an attempt was made by myself and a few other clergymen, among whom were Mr Francis Wollaston, Dr Percy, now Bishop of Dromore, and Dr Yorke, now Bishop of Ely, to induce the Bishops to promote a review of the Liturgy and Articles. ...This plan was not in the smallest degree connected with the Petition of the Feathers Tavern....We applied in a private and

perfectly well to give his Archdeaconry to Mr Bickham.[6] As to our good friend,[7] he is not in town, & talks of not being here the whole winter. Nay, Madam talks in the same manner. I should have gone to them these hollidays, if I had been well enough to stir from my fire-side. It grieves me to find that, with the other infirmities of age, the best man in the world grows captious & querulous. If you write (as I w^d have you do, sometimes) take care what you say: things affect him very differently from what they used to do.

I hope we shall see you here in the Spring, notwithstanding what you said of fixing altogether at Aston. I want to consult you on some things relating to myself, as whether I should take a house, & settle in town, & give up Thurcaston, & what I am to do with poor John,[8] whose hopes of a provision here are all blasted. But God be with you, for the present; & believe me always very cordially your's

R. H.

XXXII

HURD *to* Mason

Dear Mr Mason   *Lincoln's Inn, April 14, 1773*

Don't imagine I should have neglected you so long, if I had had a word to say to you worth making the subject of a Letter. My health, since I wrote last, has been tolerable; but that is all I have to boast of; for

respectful manner to Archbishop Cornwallis....The answer given by the Archbishop, Feb. 11. 1773 was...'nothing can in prudence be done in the matter...'".

[6] [James Bickham, a contemporary of Hurd's at Emmanuel, of which College he was Fellow and Tutor. In 1762 he was presented to the Rectory of Loughborough, and in December 1772 he was appointed Archdeacon of Leicester.]

[7] Bishop Warburton [H].   [8] His servant [H].

the town has afforded me little or no amusement. I have long since lost my relish for what are called *diversions*, & have little left even for *books*, even if the dullnefs of the present times could supply me with any, that were readible. Yes, I beg your friend Sir J[ohn] Dalrymple's pardon: his appendix is really entertaining:[1] And, if it were not for the petulant satyr on *la tête couronnée*, I might perhaps allow that the Epistle to Sir W. Chambers has its merits.[2] As to the tragical outcry of A. Stuart[3] on a good friend of mine, I must positively aver that it is very ill, as well as pafsionately written.

[1] [Sir John Dalrymple wrote *Memoirs of Great Britain from the dissolution of the last parliament of Charles II until the Sea battle of La Hogue*, of which the first part was published in 1772 and the second early in 1773. His appendixes contained a mass of political correspondence, hitherto not published, and revealed the corruption that was rife in the reign of Charles II. Walpole in a letter to Mason, of 2 March 1773 (*Letters*, VIII, p. 244), alludes to "the odious book, which is indeed as silly as it is detestable". See also Hurd to Warburton, 11 March 1773, *Letters*, p. 352.]

[2] The *Heroic Epistle to Sir William Chambers Knight, Comptroller General of His Majesty's Works, and Author of a Late Dissertation on Oriental Gardening*, was published anonymously by Mason in February 1773. Hurd was clearly not aware of Mason's responsibility for the *Epistle*, and would naturally dislike the references to George III, though the satire of them was not severe:

"Be these the royal pastimes that attend
Great Brunswick's leisure: these shall best unbend
His royal mind, when e'er from state withdrawn,
He treads the velvet of his Richmond lawn".

Mason had resigned his Chaplaincy at Court before the end of 1772. [Walpole, in a note to the *Heroic Epistle*, wrote: "It is well known that on the publication of the Heroic Epistle, his Majesty sent for it & began to read it to Sr William to laugh at him; till presently perceiving his own share in it, he threw it away in a passion". See *Satirical Poems by the Reverend William Mason with Notes written by Mr Horace Walpole in 1779*, edited by Paget Toynbee, M.A., D.Litt., Oxford, 1926.]

[3] [Andrew Stuart, a member of the Scottish bar, had been counsel for the Duke of Hamilton in the Douglas Cause, which was finally decided by the House of Lords in 1769. In 1773 he

To tell you the truth, the pleasantest part of my time this winter, has been spent among your Dowagers, to whom our good friend[4] of H[anover] Sq[uare] did me the honour to introduce me. My chief objection to them is, that, as I find from their conversation, they spoil you terribly. Out of pure kindnefs to you, I do what I can to lefsen you in their esteem; but, to say the truth, to small purpose. I even saw in the hands of one of them,[5] the etching of your Head, in an elegant purple frame, sprinkled with bay leaves (of her own workmanship) and inscribed with this motto—*As worthy of the Purple as the Bays.* Think how a Churchman & Critic, like myself, must have been shocked with this adulation!

But now, to be very serious. I believe, your advice about Thurcaston may be good: And yet, If I knew how to provide for poor Ball,[6] I should not hesitate a moment about resigning it. It w^d do no good to increase his sallary, unlefs I could ensure it to him for life....I have been looking out for a house, but have

printed *Letters to Lord Mansfield,* who, as one of the judges, had supported the claim of Archibald Douglas in whose favour the decision was given. Walpole wrote to Mason on 1 Feb. 1773: "Have you heard of Mr Andrew Stewart's *Letters to Lord Mansfield?* They will inform you how abominable abuse is, and how you may tear a man limb from limb with the greatest good breeding". *Letters,* VIII, p. 233.]

4 [Richard Hurd explains as Mr Montagu. Frederick Montagu, of Papplewick, was a friend of Mason's, but the reference is to his mother, Mrs Montagu, one of "the Dowagers", a friend of both Mason and Hurd. She was often described in the correspondence of the time as "Mrs Montagu of Hanover Square", to distinguish her from the celebrated Mrs Elizabeth Montagu, of Hill Street. Mason wrote to Alderson on 22 June 1776: "I received your letter at the Dfs of Portland's and answer if from Lady Gower's. My course of Dowagers will finish tomorrow".]

5 Mrs Delany [H].   6 His curate [H].

not sped yet, & I think shall not, the price of houses in a situation, wch I like, being more than I ought to give. But enough of this project.

Dr Balguy has carried a town cold with him to Bath, & our friend the Bp is where he has been all the winter, at Gloucester. I am to go to him at the end of June, to attend him on his visitation—What I shall do with myself afterwards, I no more know, than how the Bishops will get out of the scrape, they have brought themselves into with the Difsenters. But what care you about Bishops, when you can get your *purple* better cheap from Mrs Delaney!—As to your Whitsunday sermon, why did not you send it me, for my revisal. You had no opportunity, I warrant; as if I had not seen, &, to my shame, without remembring, & knowing again, the good & amiable countenance of your relative, & my quondam Host, Mrs Dodsworth.[7]

Adieu, my dear Sir!—tho' I should have taken my leave of you, before I had turned a new leaf, as, upon recollection, I now find that my loquacity will put you to the expence of four pence extraordinary, that is, eight pence more than twenty such sheets as this are worth. Who knows but this Letter may get in to some future collection of a Sir J. Dalrymple[8] (for afsuredly you will preserve it in your strong box at Aston) &, therefore to baulk the curiosity of malignant readers, I will conclude it without the name of your afsured friend & Servant.

[7] [Hurd's memory for names was at fault. No doubt he meant Mrs Wordsworth, a first cousin of Mason's.]

[8] Cf. Horace Walpole, *Letters*, VIII, p. 246, where Walpole writes to Mason: "Preserve this letter, and let some future Sir John Dalrymple produce it to load my memory".

XXXIII

HURD *to* Mason

Dear Mʳ Mason

Lincoln's Inn April 24, 1773

I have read your sermon with pleasure, & attention, as you will see by the frequent scratches I have made in it. You have supported your hypothesis so plausibly, that it will do excellently well for your purpose on Whitsunday. But as to printing it, I have my doubts. The *truth* of your interpretation is far from incontestible. And the *use* of it, if admitted to be true, is not so considerable, as will be expected if you make your discourse public. For the common explanation of your text leaves no room for the methodists to build their fancies upon; & the evidence, arising to Xstianity from the prophetical sense of it, is not wanted, as we have an exprefs & allowed prophecy to the same purpose from John the Baptist [Matth. iii. 11] & from Xst himself [Acts i. 5]. Still, as I said, it will be a very good Whitsunday Sermon: but I am against your printing a single discourse, unlefs it contained something not a little extraordinary. For as to the prate at court, it is not worth your minding; & it was foolish in your friends to mention it to you.

Mʳˢ Delany has a just value for you, & I must do her the justice to say, that she did not mention, or shew, the complimental bays, herself; but another of your Dowagers—not Lady Gower,[1] for my introducer conceived very reasonably, that I was not worthy of being made known to a female patriot.

---

[1] Mary, widow of the first Earl Gower, was an intimate friend of Mrs Delany and of Mrs Montagu.

86

A. Stuart's book proves nothing agst my *good friend*:[2] But this you will not believe, while you see things thro' your splenetic optics. When is it that you intend to grow—*lenior et melior, accedente senectâ*?[3]

The laureate[4] & I are just returned from an excursion to Windsor, and *Stoke*, at wch last place we indulged a melancholy hour over the grave of your late friend. This puts me in mind to tell you, how much pleased I am to hear of his life being in so great forewardneſs.[5] You will certainly not want my aſsistance: but I shall be glad to see the sheets, as they come out of the prefs. You know I shall be here till the end of June, & at Gloucester till the end of July.

As to the bon mot about Mallet,[6] it was only an observation of the Bishop's, on reading his life of Lord Bacon, where little is said of Bacon's *philosophical*, wch was his principal, character.

I have not looked into Macpherson's new translation.[7] But I can conceive very well, how he might improve Oſsian, & degrade Homer.

It may be true, as you say, that I shall never be master of a town house, & a coach: yet the former, at least, I am still hunting after. The misfortune is, that, of all those wch I have seen, the price is too much, or

[2] [In a letter to Walpole of May 7 Mason quoted what Hurd said: "I am told (by a friend of Lord M.'s indeed) that it proves nothing against his Lordship. If so I am sure nothing can be proved about any thing". *Walpole-Mason Correspondence*, I, p. 68.]

[3] [Horace, *Epistles*, II, 2, 211.]

[4] William Whitehead.

[5] [Mason was now engaged on the *Memoirs* of Gray. See L. XXXIV, n. 1.]

[6] [See L. XXXIV, n. 5.]

[7] [In 1773 James Macpherson published *The Iliad of Homer translated into Prose*.]

the situation not convenient. With, or without these paltry accomodations, you will love me, as usual, & believe me, as I truly am,

Most affectionately Yours

R. HURD

XXXIV

HURD *to* Mason

Lincoln's Inn, May 1, 1773

My dear Sir,

You are very good to take my freedoms with you so patiently. But you know that I always give you my opinion, be it good or bad, with perfect sincerity: as I am now going to do with regard to the Memoirs.

Your plan is a very good one, & the execution of it, in this specimen, agreable enough.[1] I readily conceive that the correspondence, as it proceeds, will be more manly &. important; but these juvenile Letters are entertaining, & give a natural picture of two innocent, ingenious, splenetic, young coxcombs,[2] who dote on their School-studies, think their University tutors fools, & are all the world to each other. We had something of this sort in Mʳ Shenstone's Letters:[3] but the writers wanted character, & their fancies were infantine. On the whole, I am pleased with this Section, & have nothing of moment to object to it. Only to

[1] [Mason had not yet begun to print his *Memoirs of the Life and Writings of Mr Gray*. He had sent the first pages in manuscript to Hurd.]

[2] Gray and his Eton friend, Richard West, who died in 1742.

[3] [Shenstone's *Letters to particular Friends from the year* 1739 *to* 1763 were published by Dodsley in 1769 as volume III of his *Works in Verse and Prose.*]

satisfy you the more, I will read it again carefully and put down my criticisms on a separate paper with references to the page, as I go along. When I have done this, the whole shall be transmitted to you, under Mr Frazer's[4] cover, within the time you prescribe.

This is all I have to say, at present.—As to the *bon mot*,[5] it may be somewhere in the notes on Pope, but I have not seen it there. You introduce it well, & there is no need of referring to your author.

I think as you do of the Dowagers. As for the Court, do as I do, keep your temper, & think nothing of it. You are better employed in putting together these amusing & friendly memoirs. You know me to be always, Dear Sir,

Affectionately yours

R. HURD

---

[4] [William Fraser, Under-Secretary of State, was a friend of Gray and Mason, mentioned in their correspondence. He often franked letters for them.]

[5] [Warburton originally wrote a note to Pope's *Epistle to Dr Arbuthnot*, in which he referred contemptuously to David Mallet: "He made L. B.'s life, and by ill hap forgot he was a *Philosopher*: he is now about making the D. of M.'s. Be not surprized, therefore, gentle reader, if he should forget that his Grace was a *General*". The page containing the note he cancelled. (The cancelled page is printed in facsimile in Elwin and Courthope's *Works of Pope*, vol. III, Appendix V.) Hurd had presumably seen the note in proof. The *bon mot* was current and known to be Warburton's. (See Boswell, *Life of Johnson* (Birkbeck Hill's edition), III, p. 194 and n.) Mason wanted to trace it to its source. He was quoting it at the beginning of his life of Gray: "It is said, with almost as much truth as wit, of one of these writers, that, when he composed the life of Lord Verulam, he forgot that he was a Philosopher; and therefore, it was to be feared, should he finish that of the Duke of Marlborough, he would forget that he was a General. I shall avoid a like fault. I will promise my reader that he shall, in the following pages, seldom behold Mr Gray in any other light than that of a Scholar and a Poet".]

XXXV

HURD *to* Mason

Thurcaston Oct. 18, 1773

Dear Mr Mason,

You are very good to feel so tenderly for an old friend. I wd, therefore, lose no time in letting you know, that Dr Heberden's prescription seems to have taken effect. I am considerably better, & hope in no long time to be reasonably well. My present purpose is to remove to London (by the way of Cambridge, where I am to meet R. Warburton[1]) in the first week of November.

I send Mr Bedingfield's[2] Letter under cover to M^r M[ontagu] at your house by this post. As to his criticism, I must first of all say that I totally misunderstood his meaning. By *closing elisions*, I supposed he had meant such as a verse closed with: like that in

Desuper Alcides telis premit, omnia*que a*rma
Advocat. Aen. 8.

Or, rather, like that Elision in the same page

Ecce furens animis aderat Tirynthius omnem*que*
*A*ccessum lustrans,[3]

but these instances are not frequent, &, except that variety has always a good effect in a long work, they

---

[1] Ralph Warburton, the Bishop's son. [He was born in 1756, admitted at Trinity Hall on 3 June 1773, and he died on 18 July 1775.]

[2] [Edward Bedingfield of York, a friend of Gray and Mason, assisted Mason in revising the proofs of the *Memoirs*. Letters of Mason to him on this subject are in the Henry E. Huntington Library. See Dr Toynbee's letter to the *Times Literary Supplement* of 27 May 1927.]

[3] Virgil, *Aeneid*, VIII, 249, 228.

have no great beauty. It is certain, that elisions are one great charm in Virgil's versification, but I had not observed that they were particularly affected by him in the concluding verses, or, as M.ʳ Bedingfield explains himself, *in the lines, that conclude the sense.* If the fact be so, the observation is new & curious, & should by all means be retained in the note, to w.ᶜʰ, it seems, I objected.[4]

And thus much for your ingenious friend, who writes modestly, & therefore deserves respect. But as to your own proper criticisms, I must take leave to treat them more freely. What! You took advantage of my present infirmity to be sawcy. But know that, in no state of health, do I permit a poet's petulance to go uncorrected. First, it seems, I did not know the metre of *chrystalin*:[5] Yes, I knew it full well, and should have objected to this licence in heroic verse, as it is called,

[4] [In a note (*Memoirs*, p. 160) on Gray's Latin poem *De Principiis Cogitandi* Mason gave Bedingfield's explanation: "It has already been observed in the Note on p. 36, that M.ʳ Gray's Hexameters, besides having the variety of Virgil's Pauses, closed also with his Elisions. For Virgil, as an attentive reader will immediately perceive, generally introduces one Elision, and not unfrequently more, into those Lines which terminate the Sense. This gives to his Versification its last and most exquisite grace, and leaves the ear fully satisfied. M.ʳ Gray could not fail to observe, and of course to aim at this happy effect of Elisions in a concluding Line".]

[5] Gray left six stanzas and parts of three more of an Ode, to which Mason gave the title *Ode on the Pleasure arising from Vicissitude.* Mason himself completed the Ode making use of the broken stanzas, and this version he had sent to Hurd. Hurd's criticism of "chrystalin" refers to Gray's line: "She eyes the clear crystalline well". Mason in printing the completed poem (*Poems*, p. 80) justified this by a note: "So Milton accents the word: On the crȳstalline sky, in sapphire thron'd. *P.L.* Book VI, v. 772". [Hurd's other criticisms concern Mason's additions, and Mason corrected the passages. The phrases to which Hurd objected are not to be found in the poem as Mason printed it.]

that is in such verse as Pope's & Dryden's, but not, by your leave, in a lyrical verse, wch admits of this licence, I mean when it is taken sparingly & occurs but seldom. But I am for keeping this word, because no other, under the heavens, that I know of, is so good—*transparent*, & *pellucid*, are fools to it. The 4 first verses *must* stand. With regard to the two next lines, I admit that your metre is violated by my alteration, & I was aware of it, at the time: but all I meant to suggest to you was that, *or e'er*, is insufferable in this place. It does well in David's Psalm,[6] whence you took it; but here it must not be, Mr Mason—discard me this *or e'er*, and provide for the just measure of your verse, if you will, & as you can.

But I am a fool of a critic, & am perpetually letting my candour get the better of my severity. I do admit the four lines *Happier he* &c. to be considerably better, as you have altered them. *The rich simplicity of joy*—is a little Grayish, but your lines (except that you put *high* after *flavour*, the adjective after the substantive, à la Milton, a fault I have told you of any time these twenty years) for my money.

O, you come down at last, and correct the two concluding lines very well, & just as I would have them: only, you wonder what my finical prejudice to, *of*, can arise from. But you mistake the matter; my prejudice was to TWO, *ofs*, (be pleased to look again at—Heaven's best *of* blessings)—and let me add, my prejudice is not finical, tho' it be *grammatical*. After all, Mr Bedingfield has revenged the cause of the grammarians upon you

---

[6] Psalm lviii, 8 (in the Prayer Book version): "Or ever your pots be made hot with thorns".

in his unanswerable criticisms on the two paſsages, quoted in his Letter. It is a shame for a poet to write prose so careleſsly as you do. And yet, when I say a word, I am finical. Well, but anything will do for prose, & what is not verse is nothing. Indeed, & did you never hear that good prose is rarer and more difficult (take notice, I don't say, has more merit) than good verse. I could give you in a pretty long list of good poets in our language: I defy you to mention more than two or three good prose-writers.

I nunc et versus tecum meditare canoros.[7]

I have given you, I think, for once, a pretty rattling, & should perhaps have gone on still longer in this vein, but for the most detestable pen that ever true critic scored with. What I have more to say shall be soft and sweet, like the warblings of your *celestinette*.[8]

For modesty's sake, Mr Mason, let the Ode (tho' a fine one) come in the *Memoirs*, & not in the collection of Mr Gray's *Lyrics*:[9] as to there being but eleven of

---

[7] Horace, *Epistles*, II, 2, 76.
[8] [The celestinette was a musical instrument invented by Mason. See *Walpole-Mason Correspondence*, I, p. 432, where Mason's description of it is quoted.]
[9] [It seems that Mason had suggested that the Ode, as completed by himself, might be printed in the volume of Gray's *Poems* with Gray's other Odes. If he had this intention, he took Hurd's warning to heart. Gray's six stanzas were printed in the *Memoirs*, pp. 236–7, and Mason's completed version in an appendix of *Imitations, Variations, and Additional Notes*, which he added to the *Poems* (pp. 78–81). In March 1774 he had a dozen copies of the completed Ode printed, and as he wrote to Walpole (*Walpole-Mason Correspondence*, I, p. 131), if his friends approved of its publication: "I shall print it and publish it not among his odes, no not even in the Memoirs; but only among some additional notes, which I mean to put at the end of the poems, thrown in such a place, perhaps, I may escape censure for having had the vanity to make such an attempt".]

them, *numero Deus impare gaudet*.[10] The *motto* is in the xth book of Quinctilian, and is transcribed exactly.[11] I altered *libro* to *libello*, when I inserted this pafsage in my copy, as liking the last word better.[12] But you must take no such liberties in print. I take for granted, you mean to prefix it to M[r] G.'s poems, and not to the memoirs.

Adieu, my dear Sir,
R. H.

XXXVI

HURD *to* Mason
(Part of a letter)[1]

Bloomsbury April 3, 1775

Before I conclude this letter, I must tell you there is a great mistake in your comment on a paragraph of M[r] Gray's Letter to me. You understand *the Doctor of Divinity*, there mentioned, and clafsed with *an actor*, to be D[r] Warburton. No such thing; as you might see from the date of the Letter to me, compared with the date of the other Letter cited in the note p. 250. The person, meant by Mr Gray, was Dr Brown.[2] I am sorry for this mistake, which may give pain.

[10] Virgil, *Eclogue*, 8, 75.
[11] [The quotation is from Quintilian, x, i, 94: Multum et veræ gloriæ quamvis uno libro Persius meruit.]
[12] Mason prefixed the motto to the Poems (omitting Persius and printing *libro*).
[1] This passage, copied from a letter of Hurd's by his nephew, was slipped into the Bishop's copy of Mason's *Memoirs of Mr Gray*.
[2] [In Gray's letter to Hurd of 25 Aug. 1757, which Mason printed in the *Memoirs* (pp. 249 ff.), in referring to the reception of his *Odes*, Gray wrote: "In short I have heard of no body but an Actor and a Doctor of Divinity that profefs their esteem for them". Mason in his note quotes an extract from a letter of Gray

WILLIAM MASON

INTERRUPTION OF THE CORRESPONDENCE

[NOTE. Between April 1775 and January 1788 there is a gap in the correspondence of Hurd and Mason. The interval, in part at least, coincided with a temporary breach in the friendship of the two men. Of this breach we have explicit evidence. Mason, in a letter of 5 March 1784 to his friend Christopher Alderson,[1] gives his reason for not going to town:

"I lost so many friends such as the Bp of Worcester &c some years ago, by being averse to Lord North & his American War, & I have since lost so many more by detesting Charles Fox & his vile Coalition with him that there is hardly a visit I can make in London where I shall be graciously received".

There are other allusions to his differences with Hurd. Mrs Boscawen's letter to Mrs Delany is quoted below, and in a satirical poem by Richard Polwhele,[2] Mason is made to lament:

"Alas! full oft I feel the rising Sigh
When HURD, who once could flatter, now looks shy".

We cannot be certain when the break occurred or when the friendship was resumed. In 1776 Hurd paid

to Wharton written on Oct. 7, 1757, which he says "will explain this": "D! Warburton is come to town, and I am told likes them extremely...M! Garrick's complimentary verse to me you have seen". But in August Gray had not heard of Warburton's opinion, and the "Doctor of Divinity" was Dr John Brown (see L. VIII, n. 4) as is shown by a letter to Mason of Sept. 7: "Your enemy, D! Brown, says I am the best thing in the language". Hurd's protest caused Mason to make one of the few corrections that appear in the second edition of the *Memoirs*.]

[1] [The letters of Mason to Christopher Alderson, owned by Canon R. A. Wilson, have been placed at the disposal of the editor. From these letters many of the details connected with Mason's political activities have been derived.]

[2] [*Epistle from Mr Mason to Mr Pitt*, published anonymously in 1785, and attributed to Polwhele.]

a visit to Aston, and in 1778 Mason was going to Lichfield. But by this time he had already "launched into politics".[3] He was a Whig of the old traditions, and the Ministry of Lord North brought him into antagonism to the Government and its policy. He detested the American War, and he took a leading part in the York Association, founded in 1779, which advocated parliamentary reform and the limitation of the Royal prerogative. He did not conceal his opinions in the pulpit, and his sermons were abused in the *Morning Post* and offended his Archbishop.

His standpoint and his utterances would have been distasteful to Hurd, who was a supporter of the established order and on intimate terms of friendship with the King and Queen. We know that Mason alienated others of his friends. Mrs Delany was said to have been much shocked by the political sentiments that he expressed.[4] His opposition to the Court and its Ministers must have been exaggerated, for, in January 1784, when his friend Harcourt had made his peace with the King, and when Mason's own attitude had changed, he wrote to Alderson:

"I have written this post my entire approbation of Lord H.'s Conduct & I wish you would kindly hint this to Lady Holdernesse that she may not think me so much of a Republican as I have been represented. You know nothing is further from my sentiments".

By this time the Coalition of North and Fox had

[3] [In a letter to Alderson of 13 Jan. 1777 Mason wrote: "I have launched into Politics & am likely soon to be over head & ears in them, but how and in what manner I do not think proper to explain by Letter".]
[4] [*The Autobiography and Correspondence of Mary Granville, Mrs Delany*, Second Series, III, p. 232 n.]

disgusted him, and he was in bitter opposition to their Government. This had brought him into variance with Walpole, whose friendship he lost,[5] but the way was open for a reconciliation with many of his old friends. In September 1784 the Honourable Mrs Boscawen was writing to Mrs Delany:[6]

"à propos of nouveaux convertis; I hear your friend Mr Mason is a *very* dutiful admirer of his Majesty, so *I think* he *will again* be your guest my dear madam, on a certain auspicious day next year, and meet a worthy prelate at your table. This will be *quite a restoration*, and I am glad of it; I only wish it had happen'd sooner".

There can be no doubt that Mrs Boscawen meant Hurd by the "worthy prelate" and that she looked forward to Mason meeting him at Mrs Delany's birthday party.[7]

We may therefore assume that about the year 1778 or some time later the friendship of Hurd and Mason was broken, and that in 1784, or within a little time thereafter, it was restored. The next letter that has survived is dated January 1788. From that time, at least, it is likely that there was a constant interchange of letters, and on more than one[8] occasion we know that Mason visited Hurd at Hartlebury.]

[5] [Walpole, *Letters*, XIII, pp. 124, 130. The correspondence between Walpole and Mason was resumed in 1796.]
[6] [*The Autobiography and Correspondence of Mary Granville, Mrs Delany*, Second Series, III, p. 232.]
[7] [Mason's conversion was a topic of interest to others of Mrs Delany's friends. In the autumn of 1784, when Mason was staying with Lord Harcourt, the King and Queen paid a visit to Nuneham. Frederick Montagu wrote to Mrs Delany on 22 October: "I want very much to know all the particulars of the royal visit at Nuneham, as I hear that *our poetical* friend was there. *Did he say grace? Or what did he do?*" (*Ibid.* p 235.)]
[8] [Visits in 1790, 1794, 1796 can be traced.]

XXXVII

Mason *to* Hurd

M.ʳ Mason presents his best respects to the Bishop of Worcester & desires that he would be pleased to consider this copy as a Manuscript & not permit any transcript to be taken.

York
Jan. 29 1788

[This note is written on the back page of an eight page pamphlet containing Mason's *Elegy written in a Church-Yard in South Wales*, 1787 (*Works*, I, p. 112).]

XXXVIII

Mason *to* Hurd

Aston July 19 1788

My dear Lord

I have sent the Picture this day to Sheffield according to your Lordships directions & I hope it will be forwarded to Hartlebury from Birmingham safely.

It may not be amiss to give you with it some *Notices* as Old Pegge[1] and his brother antiquarians call them of the Original. w.ᶜʰ is painted down to the knees on a three-quarter Canvas. The right hand holds a letter superscribed To Joseph Add (the rest of the word is hid by the thumb) one of his Majestys Prin*ciple* Secretarys of State. on the side is a table on w.ᶜʰ are two volumes of Rymers Fœdera.

[1] Rev. Samuel Pegge (1704–96), F.S.A., biographer of Grossetête, etc.

As the Picture belongs now to the family of the late Governor Verelst,[2] who when living could give me no other account of it <than> that it had been long an heirloom, I suspect it to be painted by Cornelius Verelst,[3] the son of Harman who was brother of Simon the famous Flower Painter whom Prior has complimented.[4] Harman who was a Portrait Painter died 1700 & left a Son Cornelius of the same Profeſsion (see Mʳ Walpoles Catalogue vol. 3, p. 34)[5] who I beleive was the Governors Grandfather.

Mʳ Addison sat to Jervas[6] for his picture in 1715 as appears from a joint Letter of Popes & Gays (see Warburtons Edition vol. 7. P. 307.)[7] two years before he was made Secretary of State. This is one Reason why I do not think Jervas Painted the Picture in question. Another is that Jervas was a Scholar & would not have written *principle*. However this be, as Mʳ Addison died in 1719 & was born in 1672, He must have been 45 or 46 when he sat for this Picture, and the Countenance of it agrees with that Age. I think that wᶜʰ your Lordship has appears much older. so much for my notices. I must however set you right in one thing that the Copy was not painted by myself,

[2] Harry Verelst, formerly Governor of Bengal [who married Ann Wordsworth, a second cousin of Mason's], acquired Aston Hall from Lord Holdernesse; he died in 1785.
[3] Son of Harmen Verelst and nephew of Simon. Died in London, 1734.
[4] [Prior, *Poems on Several Occasions*, 1718, p. 290, *A Flower*, painted by Simon Verelst.]
[5] [Mason refers to Walpole's *Anecdotes* of Painting in England.]
[6] Charles Jervas or Jarvis (? 1675–1739), pupil of Kneller, friend of Pope and Addison.
[7] [In a letter to Congreve of 7 April 1715, Gay (who wrote the first part) begins: "Mʳ Pope is going to Mʳ Jervas's, where Mʳ Addison is sitting for his picture".]

but by a Friend of mine M.ʳ Holland[8] who was of Peterhouse. I don't know whether you recollect him. I think it a very accurate Copy but you must hang it on a side light on acct of some small defect in the Canvas, w.ᶜʰ a front light only renders Visible.

I wish your Lordship may get as easily through the fatigues I find brewing for you,[9] as you did thro' the Tryal.[10] For my Part I know not w.ᶜʰ I should hold the more *penible*. M.ʳˢ Abigail says in your favorite comedy[11] "now the Coast is clear I may call in my Drummer". & so say I "that the Coast must be clear before your Lordship must call in

Your very faithful & affectionate
humble Servant
w. MASON

XXXIX

MASON *to* Hurd

York Nov. 26 1791

My Dear Lord,

I don't write to your Lordship so often as I think of you, & wish to enquire after your health, because I

---

[8] Thomas Holland, Scholar of Peterhouse, 1752, B.A. 1757; an etcher. [In R. Polwhele's *Traditions and Recollections*, I, p. 221, a letter of 28 July 1788 from R. G[reville] relates that he was taken by his friend H[olland] on a visit to Mason. He describes how "M.ʳ H. was copying a head of Addison, which M.ʳ Mason intended as a present to the Bishop of Worcester".]

[9] [Hurd was expecting the King and Queen and the Princesses to visit Hartlebury and Worcester. See his account of their visit in *Some Occurrences in my own Life*.]

[10] The trial of Warren Hastings before the House of Lords began on 13 Feb. 1788.

[11] Mrs Abigail is the servant in Addison's play, *The Drummer; or The Haunted House*. In Act I, Scene i, she says: "So now the coast is clear, I may venture to call out my drummer".

know that answering Letters is troublesome to you. and altho' I send you at present a short letter of my own, in order to inclose a very long one, I shall not expect an answer relative to either, for a reason wch will hereafter appear in the course of my Epistle.

First let me afsure you that the Person who writ the Letter gave me the copy of it, without the least guefs concerning the use I meant to make of it. I only told him I thought it was well written contained many right sentiments, & that I wished to communicate it to a friend. The writer[1] is the Son of a Parochial Clergyman in this City, who died young, & left a wife & four or five children absolutely unprovided for. I remember (about 20 years ago) that I contributed a few guineas to a subscription here, wch proved ample enough to enable his Widow to open a linnen-drapers shop, where as occasion offerd I bought my family linnen. This Son was of a studious turn, & my friend Dr Burgh[2] took a good deal of pains in preparing < him > for admittance into Clare Hall, but where he did not stay long enough to become a graduate, probably on acc^t of his finances. He has been four or five years in Priest's orders, has a small Curacy with two

[1] [From Mason's allusion below to the letters written to *The Gentleman's Magazine* "about a year ago", the young man can be identified with Thomas Watson, who was admitted a Sizar of Clare College in 1783.]

[2] William Burgh, who lived in York, was a friend and political associate of Mason. In 1783 he published a new edition of Mason's *English Garden* with Notes. [Mason left him, jointly with his Trustees, all his manuscripts in prose and verse, in the hope that Burgh would undertake the preparation of a completed edition of his works. For Burgh's neglect to fulfil Mason's wishes, see below, Appendix A, L. III*, n. 3.]

Churches near York, wch he expects to lose soon on the Death of his Rector who is very old & infirm. He has lately had the offer of a preachership in Scotland near Montrose, the profits of which are not by any means considerable & I beleive depend on contribution. He had reason to beleive from the Letter of Mr R., who advised him to come to the Place by way of probation, that Socinianism and free thinking were very fashionable in that quarter, & the Letter, wch I saw, was a very *scotch* one & led to that Idea. All this told, your Lordship will have all the Data necefsary previous to your Perusal of this his answer. His going into Scotland is still in suspense & he need not determine on the journey till next March.

In the interim, I own I am wishing (so much has the Letter prejudiced me in his favour) that some good Curacy if not some small living might be procured him in England; and I fancy that your Lordship when you have *redde*[3] it may *wish* so too, &, if you wish, you may perhaps find opportunity to fulfill our joint wish. But observe me, my dear Lord! I make no personal request. I only throw the Letter, like a Lottery ticket into a wheel, where it may pofsibly turn up a *small* prize; or from a pofsibility you may transfer it into some other ecclesiastical Wheel, where small prizes may bear a greater proportion to blanks than in your own. What may procure him, as a single man, a mere maintenance is all I aspire at for him. In vindication of my own impartiality in attempting to do him service, I will add that he is a descendant of that rank

3 For Mason's spelling *redde*, in place of read, see L. XLIII, n. 4.

Tory Bishop Watson[4] in James the $2^{d's}$ time, and the first things that brought him into my notice, were a couple of well written Letters[5] about a year ago in the Gentleman's Magazine wch he had published in vindication of his ancestor's character against some person who had attacked it. My Whigism was not strong enough to refuse giving him credit for the attempt. I remember Mr Pope in one of his Letters to Dean Swift solicits him to subscribe to Old Sam Westley's[6] comment on Job because he was a staunch Tory, & I quote his authority for my example in the present case for troubling your Lordship with a Letter, wch has run out to a much greater Length than I intended, when I sat down to write it. I am now in the first Month of a second residence wch I have had resolution to take with the hope that next summer (if not for the whole of my Life) I may have more time to visit my friends, and amongst these to visit your Lordship at Hartlebury. I am with my kind Compliments to your Nephew (who I could wish would give me a single line with regard to your Lordship's health) My Dear Lord

Your very sincere & devoted

Servant

W. MASON

[4] Thomas Watson, Bishop of St Davids, 1687–99; deprived for simony; died 1717.

[5] [The letters appeared in *The Gentleman's Magazine* for May and June 1790. In the April number, a writer "D. H." had quoted Burnet's account of Bishop Watson. Thomas Watson described himself as the nearest living relative of the Bishop and wrote to defend his memory.]

[6] Samuel Wesley, father of John. His dissertations on the book of Job were published after his death. What Pope asked Swift to do was to "propagate Mr Westley's subscription for his Com-

XL

HURD *to* Mason

Dear M.ʳ Mason

My nephew incloses to you some seeds of our oriental plant (whether rightly named by my Gardiner, I cannot say) & I take the opportunity to write one word to you.

You will see that what you said to me, when you was here, had it's proper weight with me, when I tell you that I have sent the Bp's Life[1] to the prefs. Only so many copies will be worked off as will satisfy the demands of the Purchasers[2] of the 4.ᵗʰ edition, w.ᶜʰ I think are not more than 200. So bounded is my ambition both for my friend, & for myself!

I have lately amused myself with reading again your agreable life of M.ʳ Gray. His Letters paint his character to the life. If he had been more at ease in his circumstances, & a little higher in rank, he would have been, not more estimable, but more happy.

mentary on Job, among your Divines (Bishops excepted, of whom there is no hope) ". Pope, *Works*, ed. 1769, IV, p. 348; no. XLV of the Swift letters.

[1] *A Discourse, by way of general Preface to the quarto edition of Bishop Warburton's Works, containing some account of the Life, Writings, and Character of the Author.* This was dated by Hurd: "Hartlebury Castle, August 12, 1794". [The *Life* had been written many years before. In *Some Occurrences in my own Life* Hurd wrote in 1785: "Put the last hand (at least he thinks so) to the Bishop of Gloucester's Life, to be prepared for the new edition of his works now in the prefs". The *Works* were published in 1788, but Hurd recorded: "The *Life* is omitted for the present". It was published in February 1795.]

[2] It is thus bound up in the nephew's copy of vol. 1 of the 1788 edition of Warburton's *Works* (Hartlebury Library, P. b. 6).

It will always give me a pleasure to hear from you, tho' I write but few, & short Letters myself.

With all affection, Dear Sir
Your faithful humble servant
R. WORCESTER

Hartlebury
Sept.ʳ 13ᵗʰ 1794

XLI

MASON *to* Hurd
[Copy]¹

Aston, Sep. 19, 1794

My dear Lord,

Whether on my slight suggestion, or your Lordship's better reflection you have resolved to publish your M.S. of the Bishop's Life, I feel myself highly gratified; and this not only out of my friendship for you, but the respect I have for his memory. The reason, which you some time ago gave me for withholding it from the Public eye, tho' a plausible one, did not quite satisfy me. and I must own, that had I been in your case, I shᵈ rather have with-held some what of panegyric with regard to the living Patron, than delayed what I so much owed to the dead Friend. But be this as it may, I repeat, that I am sincerely glad you have taken this resolution; for tho' I know that the petulance of periodical criticism will be as much flung forth against you now, as it would have been before, or would have been posthumously, yet of all persons in the World, your Lordship, from your present habit of life, is the most secure from being affected by it. Supposing

¹ [The original letter is not extant: but a copy in Richard Hurd's handwriting is preserved.]

that such petulance could affect you, varying the Scriptural Phrase a little, "You can stop your Ears when the *Deaf* Adder *hiſses* at you",[2] while I, who read Reviews, Magazines, Newspapers (even daily ones) & what not, frequently hear such hiſses on every side of me.

Within the course of last week I saw certain Letters of a Dᴿ Aikin (a diſsenting Physician) to his Son,[3] who hiſsed at my English Garden. I rather wondered why he was so angry; but on reading his next Letters, wᶜʰ contained strictures on Pope's Eſsay on Criticism, I found that the line in wᶜʰ we find the *dregs of Bold Socinus* was the real cause of his Spleen.[4] Hence with much self-complacency I concluded, that we shᵈ both of us have escaped censure, had we been Socinians. The very next St James's Chronicle produced me a paper signed *Impartial*, wᶜʰ accused me of Malice, Envy, &c. &c. merely because in my life of White-head[5] I had ventured to smile at the present rage for anecdote, and to mimic the turgid style of Dᴿ Johnson.

Now to such Hiſses as these, tho' I do not stop my ears, I am as little hurt by them as, I hope, your Lordship will be, shᵈ they aſsail the almost *impenetrabilia* of Hartlebury Castle.

I cannot say I quite agree with your Lordship in what you think of Mᴿ Gray. That he would have been

[2] [Psalm lviii, 4: They are as venomous as the poison of a serpent: even like the deaf adder that stoppeth her ears.]

[3] John Aikin (1747–1822), *Letters from a Father to a Son*. He was one of the editors of the *General Biography*, to which he contributed a careful article on Mason; cf. Draper, *William Mason*, pp. 5 f.

[4]   "The following licence of a Foreign reign
      Did all the dregs of bold Socinus drain."
                              Pope, *Essay on Criticism*, ll. 544–5.

[5] See L. XVII, n. 1.

more happy, had he earlier in life been in easy circumstances, is most certain, for so would every man not born to compleat competency. But an increase of Rank would have made him miserable. He had warm social affections, but he had also much natural pride, which latter had it been heightened by adventitious Rank, must have diminished the reciprocal affection of those he was most inclined to love, & this to a person of his Sensibility would have been a constant source of difsappointm! & chagrin. Of this however I am certain, that had he been superior to me (you may be afsured I mean only with respect to temporal fortune & civil Station, for in all things else I ever did & shall ever feel my inferiority) our friendship would not have continued so long as it did, & consequently your Lordship would not have been amused, as you say you have lately been, with his Letters & Memoirs by their present Editor

Believe me to be,

my dear Lord,

(with true deference to your own Rank)

Your very affectionate Friend,

w. MASON

XLII

Hurd *to* Mason

Dear M! Mason,

You are very good to think of me, &.to send me your good wishes at this season. I agree with you to think as little as I can of public affairs and to trust the great Ruler both with his earth & skies.

I really know not why the publication of this Life[1] is so long deferred. Cadell,[2] I believe, is not concerned in it, or about it. He may even be dead, for anything I know; for I have written to him twice or thrice this last year, but have been able to get no answer. The true reason of the delay I take to be this, that the printer, Mr Nicolls,[3] tho' a good man, & willing to oblige me, is almost wholly absorbed in his Magazine, & other antiquarian researches. However I expect to hear every day that the printing is finished. To prevent pirating, I have ordered the *Life* to be entered at Stationers Hall.[4] Not a single copy is printed for sale, except those which are called for by the purchasers of the Bp's Works. Of these, only 200 copies were printed; and one half of them, I believe, are not sold, to the honour of these *enlightened* times.

Having been accustomed from my infancy almost, to read only the best books, I soon acquired an indifference to general reading: and this, together with a growing indolence, has prevailed so far as to disincline me, almost, to read anything, except only that unfashionable book (the scorn of the french belles-

---

[1] Hurd's *Discourse* on Warburton.

[2] Thomas Cadell, senior, a friend of Hurd's and his neighbour in Bloomsbury, retired from the business in 1793, and died in 1802.

[3] John Nichols (1745–1823) was at this time deep in his *Leicestershire*, of which the first two parts appeared in 1795. (Hurd ordered two copies, which are still at Hartlebury.) From 1792 onwards he was sole editor of *The Gentleman's Magazine*. [Hurd in *Some Occurrences in my own Life* records in 1795 "The life of Bishop Warburton, which was sent to the prefs in Autumn last, was not printed till the end of January nor published till the end of February this year".]

[4] Hurd's instructions to Nichols about the printing and publication are given by the latter in a series of letters, *Literary Anecdotes*, VI, pp. 601 ff.

Lettres men for an age past, & now their execration)
The Bible. But your mention of two new books[5] excites
a little curiosity. I think well of their author, especially
of what is infinitely more valuable than parts & knowledge (tho' he be not deficient in these), his moral
& religious temper. I did not know he was a poet.
His subject is a pretty one for a young contemplative
mind—I shall order these two works immediately.[6]

My account of M[rs] Mainwaring is better than
your's.[7] A gentleman from Bristol wells called here
the other day, & apprehended no danger. He was a
friend, & saw her much & frequently. Her case is not
pulmonary, as he believes; & he says that her brother
had lately a complaint of the same nature, from w[ch]
he is recovered.

This is a long Letter for me. But my old habits
revive, when I have to do with an old friend. I wish
you health & ease, &, what is almost better than
happinefs, at least may supply the place of it in this
world, that composure of mind w[ch] I thank God I
enjoy in this solitude. My nephew, who is a great comfort to me, has a particular respect and esteem for you.

Adieu, my dear Sir,

Your affectionate friend &

Hartlebury Castle   servant

Jan. 2. 1795   R. WORCESTER

[5] The Bishop's nephew adds: "Walks in a Forest and The Inquiry &c by the Rev. Thomas Gisborne". They were both issued
in 1794. The full title of the latter is "An Inquiry into the Duties
of Men in the Higher Ranks & Middle Classes of Society in Great
Britain". It went through six editions and the "Walks" through
eight. The author was a friend of Mason. See L. XXXV.
[6] The Bishop's copy of the "Inquiry" remains in Hartlebury
library; but not the poems.   [7] [See L. XLVI, n. 4.]

XLIII

Mason *to* Hurd

Aston March 26 1795

My dear Lord,

It was but four days ago, that I rec^d your pre-
liminary Discourse;[1] for wishing to receive it safer than
by common conveyance, I desird a Gentleman in this
neighbourhood to bring it down from Mr Stonhewer,[2]
who had before procured it for me from Robson the
bookseller, & this Gentleman instead of staying in
London a week did not return of three: otherwise I
should have written to your Lordship sooner, as I had
promised.

I have redde it, according to Bp Horsley's,[3] but not
your Orthography, with much care, & yet to me,
whatever it may have to your Lordship,

It has no faults, or I no faults can spy.[4]

I mean with respect to style, manner, and all that
relates to the Bps own character; with respect to the
Character of others incidentally drawn I also agree
with you more than the present race of Readers will:

[1] The *Discourse* on Warburton's life; see L. XL, n. 1.
[2] [Richard Stonhewer, elected Fellow of Peterhouse in 1751,
was an intimate friend of both Gray and Mason. He became
private secretary to the Duke of Grafton, whose private tutor he
had been at Cambridge, and held various offices under Government. He was one of the Trustees of Mason's will, and to him
Mason left Gray's books and manuscripts. See Appendix A,
LL. II*, n. 3, III*.]
[3] E.g. S. Horsley, *Letters to Dr Priestley* (1784), p. 39: "Had you
redde it through". Mason adopted the spelling.
[4] [Prefixed to Mallet's *Truth in Rhyme* (1761) was an "*Imprimatur*" by Lord Chesterfield:

It has no faults, or I no faults can spy,
It has all beauty or all blindness I.]

& I admire evry part of the work, in wch you have shewn the least degree of Prudence, & consequently the highest degree of downright declaration of your own Sentiments. This became the Biographer of Warburton, & in this you have answered my Expectation to the full.

Your Lordship knows I always differd with you with respect to a favorite Hypothesis of yours, that Genius has a precise time for coming to its *acme*, or at least decreases sooner than the corporeal faculties, & this, I know, you imputed long ago to our excellent friend & have now publicly avowed it.[5] For my own part, I think his unfinished ninth book is an instance to the contrary; for there is more of original, I will not say uncontrovertible, thinking in that Book than in almost any thing he has written, & expressed with as much force. The most paradoxical part of it, respecting the fall, is surely ingenious in the highest degree. But that it is more than ingenious I say not. However such original thought could not have enterd into any Man's brain, whose imagination & Fancy had been by Time impaired. I know your Lordship & I shall never agree on this point, yet as I have been so long in the habit of speaking my mind to you as well (to my own detriment perhaps) as to all the world, I trust you will forgive me. I have done so lately to a very learned Chaplain of my Lord of Durham's,[6] a Mr Burgess,[7]

[5] The reference is to the comments in Hurd's *Discourse* (p. 98) on the defects of book IX of the *Divine Legation*: "His faculties, hitherto so bright and vigorous, suffered some eclipse and diminution of their force, from his growing indispositions".

[6] Shute Barrington.

[7] Thomas Burgess, afterwards Bishop of Salisbury.

who sent me a private printed copy of the Epistola ad Pisones, every sentence of wch was most licentiously transposed, because, Forsooth!, he & his brother Chaplain had agreed that "in its first form it was more immethodical than the Epistolary style permitted". But I gave him a Rowland for his Oliver, as our good Bishop would have said & done, & hope on this acct to be set down as a true Pupil of the Warburtonian School by the Prelate himself. But to return to a better subject. I am heartily rejoiced that your Lordship has given this finish to an Edition, wch would have been imperfect without it, & that you have finished it in a way, w^ch, when Prejudice has had its day, will be as honorable to your own memory as that of our illustrious friend.

Believe me to be with compliments to your Nephew and with the sincerest Respects to yourself

My dear Lord,

Your very affectionate Servt

W MASON

I have a great mind to fill up the remainder of this Paper with a Septuagenarian-Petrarchian Sonnett, wch I wrote last month on my Birthday, tho' I know you will condemn it, because it was written full thirty years after a Poet should have left off writing.[8]

[8] There follows Mason's Sonnet vii (*Works*, i, p. 128) as Mason originally wrote it. For Hurd's criticism and Mason's correction, see LL. XLIV, XLV. The sonnet when published bore the title: "February 23, 1795 Anniversary". In the copy sent to Hurd, Mason added at the foot: "Feb: 12th O.S. 1795". ["Old style" refers to the change in the day of the month.]

XLIV

Hurd *to* Mason

My dear Sir

Your Letter of the 26th past, crofsed one of mine to you—I cannot but be much pleased with your approbation of the *Life*, because I know you always tell me your real sentiments. I have reason to believe that the characters of Secker & Lowth[1] are not relished by your friend the Bp. of London,[2] and by the family, or schools rather, of W. of Wickham.[3] Nor could anything else be expected from either quarter.

Your account of the Durham critics is pleasant enough. Who is this *Sturges*?[4] He must be a poor creature to have recourse to such licentious transpositions for the vindication of his author. His patron,[5] I believe, means well; but so much vanity is never attended by true judgment.

I rejoice to hear that you have no complaints to make of old age. To me, it's depredations are very

---

[1] The references to Secker and Lowth are on pp. 82 f. and 94 f. of the *Discourse*. [Hurd wrote to Bishop Butler on April 20, 1795: "As to Bishops Secker and Lowth, I have not only been just but civil to them. Yet it will not surprise me to find that their blind admirers think otherwise". Kilvert, p. 327.]

[2] [Beilby Porteus (appointed Bishop of London in 1787) was on friendly terms with Mason, perhaps from his Cambridge days, where he was in residence at Christ's College, as a Fellow, for ten years. Their friendship is shown by the letters which passed between them, referred to in LL. XLVIII, XLIX below, and by an unpublished letter which the Bishop wrote to Christopher Alderson on receiving the news of Mason's death.]

[3] Lowth and Burgess, and Henry Addington, his patron, were Wykehamists.

[4] The Bishop misread Burgess in Mason's letter. See L. XLIII, n. 7.   [5] Apparently Bishop Barrington.

sensible. As to the general question, I perceive, we are not likely to agree. But in the particular case of the ix^{th} book,[6] we differ lefs than you imagine. The matter of that book is, as you observe, as original & ingenious, as anything he ever wrote. But then you are to reflect, that the *matter* had been laid in and digested, in his better days. The *composition*, tho' of wonderful merit, as I observe, all circumstances considered, is yet inferiour to that of the other books; such notes & pafsages only excepted as he had written long before. On the whole, there are exceptions to the general Rule, but it holds good for the most part. At least, I think so.

But now for the Septuagenarian Sonnet. I like it extremely well, both sentiment & exprefsion. The only criticisms I have to make upon it, are 1. that *reign* in v. 8 does not rhyme well with *men*.[7] 2 *That* silent lay, That musing gratitude v. 11 & 12. The second *that*, should be *which*. 3. I have fancied that in the last line *And praise with more than tongue*—might be ex-prefsed more happily.[8]

Take notice, I do not forbid your writing a sonnet, now & then, or any short poem. But a long work of invention, another Georgic, for instance, or dramatic poem, I shall not allow you to undertake at 70.

This deanery[9] yet hangs. I know not why unlefs these stirs in Ireland have occasioned any delay. D^{r}

[6] [See L. XIII, n. 5.]
[7] Mason stuck to *reign*. He accepted the next suggestion.
[8] The last line of the sonnet was:

"And praise with more than Tongue, my God and King".
For Mason's substitution, see L. XLV.
[9] I.e. of Worcester. Dr St Andrew St John died 23 March 1795. Dr Arthur Onslow, nephew of Speaker Onslow, was in-stalled May 16.

Evans' dependance, if he thinks of it at all, can only be on the Duke of Portland.[10]

With my nephew's best respects, & my fervent wishes that you may live to write many more birth-day Sonnets, I am ever, Dear Sir,

Your affectionate humble servant

R. WORCESTER

H.C. Ap. 8ᵗʰ 1795

XLV

MASON *to* Hurd

[*York, Aug. or Sept. 1795*][1]

My dear Lord,

I have been most shamefully remiſs in not writing to you of so many months, but the truth is I have for many months been much indisposed with indigestion, flatulency, & nervous feelings wᶜʰ have depreſsed my spirits extreamly, so that I have written no Letters except on immediate buſineſs. I have however lately began with an infusion of Quaſsia, a strong bitter, wᶜʰ from the good effect I have already experienced seems to promise, under providence, a cure of my complaint.

I beleive I promised your Lordship a present of my slight Musical Eſsays,[2] & that afterwards, when I had resolved on making no present on acct of my numerous acquaintance, I forgot to apologize for having withdrawn my Promise. So that probably you have never

---

[10] Then Home Secretary.
[1] Mason did not date the letter. Richard Hurd endorsed it "from York about Augᵗ or Sept. 1795". [It is a reply to Hurd's letter of April 8 (L. XLIV).]
[2] [*Essays, Historical and Critical on English Church Music* had been published in February 1795.]

seen them. If so there is little harm done, for by what I find they are mighty likely to pafs thro' the world unnoticed.

I have been two months residing in this dullest of all dull places, & have lost the comfort of the late uncommonly fine Autumn, with nothing to do (as the ceiling of our Cathedral is stuccoing) but to chaunt the second Service on a Sunday; The want of a proper substitute obliges me to this.

Your Lordship disliked the last line of my Sonnet. Pray substitute this in its place

—shall Faith convey
And Hope the Cherub of unwearied Wing.

By wch I mean to exprefs, in the Sonnet style, what Pope has in the Didactic

Hope travells thro nor quits us when we die.[3]

This Letter, short as it is, is the longest I have written of some time for in a morning my hand has been hardly able to direct a pen tho now much better. It is written merely to hope for a line from your good Nephew (for I feel as if I was unworthy to receive one from yourself) to know *si valeas* that I may say from my heart *Bene est* in hope that I may finish the Sentence[4] in my next Letter, from My Dear Lord

Yours truely and affectionately

W. MASON

[3] [Pope, *Essay on Man*, II, l. 274.]
[4] [Mason has in mind the common form often found at the beginning of Cicero's *Letters*, SVBE EQV. He hopes to be able to say *Ego quoque valeo*, when he writes again.]

XLVI

MASON *to* Hurd

Aston Nov. 11 1795

My dear Lord,

I deferrd answering your Lordship's obliging Letter, till I had returned to this quiet Place, altho' while I was at York, having no call to Cathedral Service save on Sundays on account of reparations going on in the roof of the Church, I had more leisure, & consequently comfort, than I ever had before, whò for above thirty years had been, what your favorite Cowley calls *the Pupil of a Bell.*[1] I had also more opportunity of attending to my Health; having had leſs necefſity to see much company. and the regular use I have made of the medicine, I mentioned before, has, I thank God for it, done me very considerable service, tho' my Stomach is not yet quite so easy as it was formerly, w.ᶜʰ makes it necefſary for me to be careful in point of Diet. Quafſia is a root or Wood, w.ᶜʰ comes from Surinam, of w.ᶜʰ so much has of late years been imported, that it is the cheapest of all medicines &, what is still better, incapable of being adulterated. it is the purest of all Bitters & the lightest. the Swiſs Physician Tiſsot, in his Eſsay Sur la santé des Gens de Lettres page 223, Printed at Lausanne 1768, when it was then rather a new drug, praises it highly, & thinks it preferable, except in febrile cases, to the Bark, w.ᶜʰ a sensible Man of the faculty tells me is now so apt to be adulterated, that they can seldom depend on its efficacy. The College,

[1] Cowley, *Ode upon Liberty*, c. 5 (Hurd, *Cowley,* 3rd ed. (1777), II, p. 116):
"Unhappy slave, ànd pupil to a bell".

I beleive, for the first time have adopted it here in their last Pharmacopeia.[2] My mode of taking it is this. A quarter of an ounce of the Chips is put into a Pint Bason, on which a pint of Boiling Water is pour'd, in three or four minutes it is sufficiently bitter, & when strained or rather run thro a Seive & suffered to cool. then adding a spoonful of Brandy to three large spoonfuls of the infusion, wch. is as clear as Water, I took it twice a day before noon & after. This mode was prescribed to me for the first week; but since, it stands on the Water till quite cold, wch. I think does not add much to its Bitter taste, & I now use it without the Brandy. I am thus particular about it, as I wish your Lordship would try it as, I beleve, it <is> at least perfectly safe, yet I would not recommend it except your Scotch D^r at Worcester, whose name I have forgot (O it is Johnson or Johnston)[3] should afsent to it. for I do not know what effect it may have on your Lordships *Ganglions*.

I had a Letter since I came here from Poor Mainwaring[4] who, I am glad to find, is returned to Cambridge & in tolerable Health. He tells me that both you & himself have redde my little musical Efsays, & afsent to my general Doctrine so far as you understand. I thought I had written sufficiently popularly

<hr />

[2] Quassia was officially recognised in the *London Pharmacopoeia* of 1788.

[3] James Johnstone, M.D. Edinburgh, practised in Kidderminster and Worcester, and his nephew John in Birmingham. Their *Medical Essays & Observations* on the Ganglions of the Nerves, etc. (1771, 1795) were presented "to the Right Reverend Richard Lord Bishop of Worcester from his Lordships much obliged humble Servants the Authors".

[4] John Mainwaring, of St John's, Cambridge, Lady Margaret Professor of Divinity 1788–1807. See L. LI, n. 5. [His wife had died in June of this year.]

for those, who were musical Dilettanti like you both. Yet not for my friend Gilpin,[5] who tells me he consulted Johnson's Dictionary & found that Counterpoint *was a quilt woven in Squares* by wch you see that Colofsus of Etymology mistook the term for Counterpain.[6] He next wanting to know what Difference there was, if any, between Melody & Harmony, found me all in the wrong, for the Lexicographer told him that *Melody is Harmony.*[7] for such readers & such expositors I certainly did not write.

I am dayly in expectation of my friend Dixon,[8] wch this story will amuse, if it does not you. I hope he will stay with me some time. Believe me to be, My Dear Lord,

Your affectionately devoted Servant

W. MASON

My best compliments attend your Nephew

[5] Rev. William Gilpin (1724–1804), a voluminous writer on a great variety of subjects. Hurd possessed his lives of Cranmer and Wycliffe and other works.

[6] Mason should have consulted the Dictionary himself. Johnson, indeed, says nothing of the musical associations of counterpoint, but he made no mistake:

Counterpane *n.s.* [*Contrepoint,* French] . . . . It is sometimes written, according to etymology, *counterpoint.*
Counterpoint *n.s.* A coverlet woven in squares, commonly spoken *counterpane.*

[7] This, again, is not just. Johnson says that melody is "Musick; sweetness of sound". He does say: Melodious *adj.* (from *melody*). Musical; harmonious. But Mason would scarcely find fault with his definition of harmony as "just proportion of sound; musical concord".

[8] [The Reverend John Dixon (whose brother Henry married Mason's half-sister Ann), Rector of Boughton, Northants, was an intimate friend of Mason, and one of the trustees of his will. There are references to him in later letters, and letters from him in Appendix A, LL. III*, V*.]

XLVII

MASON *to* Hurd

Aston Jan. 25 1796

My dear Lord,

I am conscious that I have deferred answering your
Lordship's last very obliging Letter much longer than
I ought to have done, but instead of making apologies,
wch are always tedious both to the writer & the reader,
I shall only say, what I trust you will candidly admit,
—better late than never.

Your defence of Musical Creeds[1] is ingenious, but it
rather comes ill from a Clerk of his Majesty's Closet,[2]
& wch I should not admit even from a Dean of his
Chappel. the Truth is, that the Apostle's Creed, I
beleive, never was set to Music, tho the Nicene has,
& is so performed in many Cathedrals, but not in the
Chappel of the supreme head of the Church of England.
When I had the honour to be a Chaplain, I noted this
& approvd it, having always found that the Har-
monical Music it was set to rendred it absolutely unintelligible; on this acct, when I was well with the
Dean of York[3] & a kind of Prime Minister to him,

---

[1] The loss of Hurd's letter is regrettable. In reading Mason's
essays on Church Music he must have found the note in which
(*Works*, III, p. 351) the Precentor deprecates the inclusion in com-
posers' "services" of settings of the Nicene Creed: "In my opinion
any Music whatever is improper to accompany a solemn declaration of our Faith.... Creeds are and must be, of necessity, narrative". Clearly, Hurd defended the other view.

[2] [Hurd was appointed "Clerk of the Closet" when he was
translated to Worcester.]

[3] John Fountayne, who was Dean of York from 1747 to 1802.
[To him Mason owed his appointment as Canon Residentiary.
See Appendix A, L. II*, n. 1.]

I persuaded him, quoting my regal Authority for it, to have it simply *redde* & instead of two unmeaning Voluntarys a fine Sanctus of D.ʳ Boyce's performed going & coming from the communion Table, for w.ᶜʰ also I had the same Authority: and so in our Minster it continues still to be.⁴ But indeed, my good Lord, you seem to carry your cautious & temperate Ideas of reform almost as far as your Old Brother Beveridge, who writ a tract,⁵ w.ᶜʰ I once saw, against Tate & Brady's new version of the Psalms, because it was too refined & Poetical, & most manfully and Episcopally & Orthodoxly defended Old Thomas Sternhold. I remember, when the Nicene Creed was sung at York, It was usual for the Dean or Officiating Residentiary to chaunt audibly "I believe in one God" —& then the Organ & Choir took up in their Counterpoint & Canon the rest of it. On w.ᶜʰ some wag, who I suppose, suspected the Chaunter to be a Socinian, said "& I fancy you believe no more" & if the said Officiating Prebend, as I think he was, was a relation of Archbishop Herring's he perhaps made a good guefs. So much then for the subject of Musical *Credos*, for that is the musical term.

A very excellent Woman with whom I had long been acquainted died last Month, after suffering more than fourteen years in a peculiar species of Atrophy attended with much pain & an entire lofs of strength in evry limb, but retain'd her Memory & intellects, w.ᶜʰ were great, even to the last. I had promised her many years

⁴ It would seem that the Precentor must persuade the Dean before such a change could be made.
⁵ William Beveridge (Bishop of St Asaph), *Defence of the Book of Psalms*, 1710.

ago to write her Epitaph, wch I have lately done, tho'
from a much earlier Idea, & your Lordship will oblige
me much if you will give me your Critique upon it,
as I wish to make it as perfect as I am able. As besides
her moral & truly Christian Character, she was
eminent in copying Pictures with her needle, this
Talent, wch was at the time almost new and singular,
requird to be noticed. Therefore I thought it necefsary
to borrow aid from Scripture & the design of the
Monument, wch is of the kind they call Mural, is to be
an antique female figure working on a frame, & an
Easel before her with an original *Canvas* on a painter's
Easel[6] under this Alto Releivo on the front of a Cinerary
Vase the following inscription on a plain marble tablet.

To the Memory

of Mrs Ann Moritt[7] &c.—

While sculptord Marble on this Wall displays
Her Skill to emulate the Pencil's praise,
To seize the Painter's powers without the name,
And soar on female attribute to Fame,
This Verse records how to those powers were join'd
The strongest, manliest energies of mind;
Witness the years of Pain her frame sustain'd
With Patience firm, with fortitude unfeignd
And heaven-aspiring Hope;—what need of more,
For Faith & Charity were her's before?

Every body that knew her will say nothing here is
exaggerated, Particularly her uncommon soundnefs of
Judgment, wch was of the masculine cast.

[6] [Mason's statement is confused. The sense requires a stop
after "a painter's Easel": and "a painter's Easel" merely repeats
"an Easel before her".]
[7] [The Epitaph (with many alterations from the first version)
is Epitaph VIII (*Works*, I, p. 144). Mrs Ann Morritt was of the
family which owned Rokeby Park, Yorkshire.]

I wish much to have your Lordship's early opinion of these lines, because I know not how soon I may be called upon for them.

My friend Dixon has left me for Buxton by the advice of a physician in this neighbourhood, in order to fix a flying Gout, wch has of late attacked his Bowels. I hope to see him again on his return, & I hope with improvd Health. for myself, God be thanked, I never was better, I went through a course of Quafsia for six weeks, wch I was ordered to repeat after a month, The interval I filld up with a dayly pint of Tar Water, and am now in my second Course of Quafsia, tho hardly necefsary. I wish Dr Johnson, who I find has edited his ganglions afresh, may put your Lordship in the same regimen, & this the rather because Quafsia is incapable of Adulteration. Whereas I am told by the Faculty that Bark is now seldom to be met with genuine.

I inclose a line to my good friend your Nephew on a very different subject concerning wch I doubt not he will give me his best advice & afsistance.[8] Hoping that this wonderfully mild, tho somewhat boisterous, Winter, if the two terms be not incongruous, has agreed with you.

I conclude with perfect respect

Your Lordships truely affectionate,
W. MASON

[8] [From the next letter it appears that Mason was seeking information about hand-mills.]

XLVIII

MASON *to* Hurd

My dear Lord

I am sorry that your Nephew's enquiries concerning Hand mills did not turn out so satisfactorily as I had hoped. I am however much obliged to him for the intelligence. Unleſs something can speedily be done to stop that spirit of Speculation, wᶜʰ has now spread from the richest Merchants to the mere Farmers &c, & from Commerce to Agriculture, actum est, I will not say *de* republica, but *pro* Republica, taking it in the french acceptation of the Word, that is Britain will become a French Republic.

A Post before I recᵈ your Lordship's last favour, I recᵈ one from My Lord of London,[1] wᶜʰ amongst other literary chit chat such as the new forgery of Shakespeare[2] &c mentions the Oxonian attack[3] on you. He speaks civilly of your Lordship, as all Bishops should do & *always do* one of another, yet own'd " he was hurt at what you said of his Old Friend & Patron[4] &

---

[1] Beilby Porteus. See L. XLIV, n. 2.

[2] [William Henry Ireland had exhibited his forged manuscripts in 1795, and in December had printed his documents. They were being attacked and exposed in the newspapers.]

[3] [In January 1796 there was published *A Letter to the Lord Bishop of Worcester occasioned by the Strictures on Archbishop Secker and Bishop Lowth in his Life of Bishop Warburton, now prefixed to his Quarto Edition of that Prelate's Works. By a Member of the University of Oxford.* The authorship was subsequently avowed by the Rev. Thomas Wintle, of Pembroke College, Oxford, see n. 5 below.]

[4] Porteus was made domestic chaplain to Archbishop Secker in 1762. Secker, he said, was to him "a most kind friend and a bountiful benefactor". He had the benefit "of being honoured with his direction and advice, and of living under the influence of his example". (R. Hodgson, *Life of Porteus*, pp. 16 f.)

thought it would produce an answer from some Quarter or other ". For obvious reasons I thought it best to answer this Letter sooner than our usual course of Correspondence requird, & I have got my Friend Dixon, who is now with me, to transcribe that part of my Letter, & his Copy I enclose. It will at once please you, & offend you, please you, because I am confident it speaks your own Sentiments about Hebrew literature; and offend you, because it is written in a more flippant way, than even a Bishop would dare to write to a Bishop. To say the Truth, when I consider, that he is almost the only Bishop (excepting your Lordship who at my instance made Dixon your temporary Chaplain) who ever shewd me the slightest favour, whereas one at least if not more have done me personal injury—Whereas Bishop Porteus has lately appointed two White hall Preachers from Cambridge at my request; therefore in Gratitude I ought to have treated him with more deference. How His Lordship will take it I know not, yet it is my custom to speak my mind in Season and out of season & abide all consequences. And I should be a fool at my time of Life to practice a Prudence, wch could but little avail either myself, or the few friends whom I might wish to serve by it.

The Pamplet I have since seen, Mr Stonhewer having sent it me in Covers at my request. and he tells me that it is given to a Dr Blaney, a Canon of Christ Church,[5] who published *a la Lowth* a version of Jere-

[5] Bishop Hurd adds a note: "The Pamphlet, alluded to, was certainly not written by Dr Blaney". His nephew adds in pencil: "The Writer was the Rev. Mr Wintle of Pembroke College, Oxford". See n. 3.

miah.[6] Dixon tells me he is of so sanguine Irascible a temper, that he has been nicknamed Devil Blaney,[7] tho' in this pamphlet he seems to have tryd to metamorphose himself into an Angel of Light, & to affect a species of Candor w^{ch}, whenever I see it, gives me the same sensations as an Emetic.—After all, 'tis a miserable Businefs, and did I think it worth while I would (as *our* Bishop said of a certain noble writer) " *be among his Potts* ", or among his Hebrew roots, wch are of the same sort of Crockery ware, with this difference that the ware is to be used before it has been in the Oven, when it is so pliable you may twist it as you please. Happy is it, that it has hitherto been in the hands of such clumsy Potters, that they have hardly known how to twist it at all.

I come in the last place to thank your Lordship for your strictures on the epitaph, and shall in defference to them substitute the word *Industry* for *Attributes*,[8] excellence being, in my mind, too general a term, and the Art of Copying Pictures in Needle work is rather a mark of Industry than Genius, wch excellence rather implys. But with respect to the last line & half I am obligd to be restive.[9] First, because the Faith &

[6] Benjamin Blayney, D.D., was Regius Professor of Hebrew 1787–1801. Hurd possessed a copy of Blayney's *Jeremiah*, 1784, and received a copy of the same writer's *Zechariah*, 1797, "from the Author".

[7] "This malignant nickname," Hurd notes, "was certainly misapplied."

[8] [Mason wrote "attribute" in the copy sent to Hurd (L. XLVII): in the published version he had "attributes" (not "industry").]

[9] [Hurd maintained his objections, as appears in the next letter. Mason was then resolved not to change, but in October 1796 (see L. LII) he submitted a new version of the last four lines, and this, with some further changes, was ultimately adopted.]

Charity of the Deceased were remarkable & therefore required to be recorded, & what says the Epitaph except that after a Life, in wch she had exercis'd these two Christian Virtues, she supported the conclusion with two others Patience and Hope, when in a long state of extreme Pain before her difsolution. If it exprefses this latter part quaintly it cannot be helped. I am sure it exprefses it simply & even prosaically, & if it be like Cowley it ill becomes the editor of Cowley [10] to animadvert upon it, a Writer, who, in my Opinion, had little other merit than that of being a good, tho' unsuccefsful Courtier to a flagitious Prince. This, however, at the Time, was what might be deemed laudable Loyalty. Heaven Send! that after our Time, some future Poet may not be forced to play the same Game; in order to counterwork Democracy, as he did out of a just hatred to Puritanism & Hypocricy—Dixi—

Believe me My Dear Lord to be

most cordially yours

W. MASON

XLVIII *a*

MASON *to* Bishop Porteus

Feb. 3 1796

(Extract)

I own I rather wonder, that your Lordship should be either concerned or hurt at the Paragraph in the Life of Warburton, which contains the Editor's opinion of A Bp Secker. I have since looked not only into that offensive paragraph, but into that concerning Bishop

---

[10] [In 1772 Hurd published *Select Works of Cowley* with preface and notes.]

Lowth, which I imagined when I first saw it, would give more offence. With respect to the former, he gives[1] the A Bp the merit of being "a wise Man, an edifying Preacher & an exemplary Bishop", three things that any Bishop, I think, might deem sufficiently to the credit of even an Archbishop, & wch I, who did not know Dr Secker, could not in conscience have given *in full* to any Archbishop that in the course of a long life has come within my cognisance. Had he said, which he does not, that he had not so original a Genius as Warburton, I think there are few but those who are highly prejudiced against Warburton, who would not aſsent to that opinion. But he only says, "that the course of his life (a very public one) and his studies had not qualified him to decide on such a work as the Divine Legation". For myself I think, that whether he was capable of deciding or not, his Prudence would have prompted him not to decide, when encircled with such a set of Bishops & other dignified Ecclesiastics, almost universally Warburton's enemies, who in the Duke of Newcastle's time were promoted either thro' Borough-interest, or that of the University, which the Duke prided himself of as being his absolute borough. But it seems the Bishop of Worcester has called Hebrew literature a *narrow walk*; this, I think, cannot affect your Lordship, who so far as my opinion goes has done wisely in not walking in it. Were I to compare it to any thing, it would be to Mr Uvedale Price's[2] picturesque

---

[1] Hurd, *Discourse* (1794), p. 82.
[2] Of Foxley, Hereford. His *Essay on the Picturesque* was published in 1794. He was made a baronet in 1828 and died in 1829. Price contends that the features of a lane, especially if it be through a park leading up to a great house, should be "variety" and

lane, where a man cannot pass without bruising his shins in quarry holes, or stinging them with nettles (Pray do not tell either my Lord of Durham,[3] or M[rs] Kennicott[4] that I say so). But your Lordship must have already seen from my slight musical Efsays[5] my sentiments on that subject, tho' there I somehow or other contrary to my usual practice preserved a kind of sage *retenu*: yet in such a familiar letter as this, & knowing also to whom I write it, I will venture to be still more open, & own to you, that I go further than Butler, the Rhymer, (not the Bishop, on whom your good Patron[6] bestowed so much laudable pains), for I am so far from thinking with him that Hebrew Roots grow best on barren ground,[7] that I have not yet found reason to think that they flourish on any ground at all. After I have said this, I should tire your Lordship's patience, were I to expatiate on the other character. Instead of doing so, I will give you an Anecdote. When D[r] Parr published his now-forgotten Preface to Bellendenus,[8] The Westminsters and

"intricacy"; to which Sir T. Dick Lauder, who produced an edition of *The Picturesque* in 1842, replied that what he liked was to feel the drive to be smooth and level under the carriage as it "bowls on its way up to the portal of the mansion" (p. 75).

[3] Shute Barrington, to whom Blayney dedicated his *Jeremiah*.

[4] Anne, sister of Edward Chamberlayne; she was married to Kennicott in 1771.

[5] Mason is referring to the third musical Essay "on Parochial Psalmody" (*Works*, III, pp. 363 ff.).

[6] The relations of Secker to Butler are noted in A. E. Baker, *Bishop Butler* (S.P.C.K.), pp. 24 f., 27, 36, etc.

[7] S. Butler, *Hudibras*, part I, canto 1, l. 59 f.:
"For Hebrew roots, although they're found
To flourish most in barren ground,..."

[8] William Bellenden, the Scotsman who became a professor at the University of Paris, and wrote three treatises on Roman political history. They were combined in one large volume, *De*

Etonians were all in raptures about its latinity.
I remember I said to one of them who was of the very
ministerial Party, which he had abused: "Were it
worth while, I would translate it into the best
English I could, in order to show its futility". a few
weeks after I saw a very good translation of it in a
Newspaper, & what was it? One of the poorest
tritical eſsays, that ever appeared in a Newspaper.
Methinks my Lord I see you ready with an application, & crying What? Compare Dᖴ Parr & Dᖴ
Lowth together! No, by no means: all I would have
you infer is, that elegant claſsical latinity is the best
veil in the world for a scarcity of sense, & a weakneſs
of argument: If you wish for a proof, see Mᖴ or Dᖴ
Gregory's version, & certainly a correct one, of certain
celebrated Lectures.[9] I dare say the book is in your
Lordship's Library, & most probably unread. For
my part, had I been capable of writing those Lectures,
I should have wished to have anathematized any
Person, who dared to translate them out of an idea of
doing me honour, & would sooner have borne with
severer strictures than either Hurd or Warburton could
have given me. But truce with this subject which as
coming from one, tho' the lowest, of the Warburton
School, you will treat as you think it deserves, & fling
into the fire.[10]

Statu Libri Tres, in 1615. This "forgotten" work was recalled to
notice by Parr's "now forgotten" preface to his edition of 1787.
The *Prefatio* was translated by William Beloe in 1788.
[9] Lowth's *Prælectiones de Sacra Poesi Hebræorum,* 1753, were translated into English by George Gregory, 1787. The "Mᖴ or Dᖴ"
refers to the fact that Gregory, a minister of the Kirk, was D.D.
Edinburgh, 1792.
[10] Even among Hurd's friends there were those who did not
take Mason's view of the Secker-Lowth passages in the *Discourse.*

XLIX

Mason *to* Hurd

Aston Feb. 25th 1796

My Dear Lord,

If I had expected that the extract of my flippant Letter would have been so candidly, not to say favorably rec^d, I should have desird my friend Dixon to have copied the whole of it; for as far as I remember[1] what I said of the other Prelate was still more flippant. Yet the Bishop, to whom I addrefsed it, seems vastly pleased with it, & wishes to receive many more such *lively* Letters from me. And as His Archbishop said, as I have heard, at his public Table to a Person who said a certain old Lady desired his Prayers "Good Woman she shall have them", so will I indulge him with my *Livelinefs*. I recollect however that I compared Lowth's Lectures to Parr's preface to Bellendenus, & said that, stript of their Latinity, they were equally meagre in point of sense. And this I said, on the authority of my Curate, whose opinion I would trust as soon as any Man's on such a subject. He had never seen the said Lectures in the Original. M^r or Dr Gregory, who had translated them, & had sent me a Copy a few years ago, because I had civilly, at his request, suffered him to publish my Ode from Isaiah[2] in them, and this Book

Hurd has added to the title-page of *Remarks on the Pursuits of Literature in a Letter to the Author* (Cambridge, 1798) the words "By Mr Professor Mainwaring". "I am one of those", says the writer, p. 8, "who sincerely wish that the Bishop of Worcester had abstained from some observations which justice seemed to require, for a full and perfect display of such a character as Warburton"; see also p. 11.

[1] [What Mason said of Lowth had been included in the extract sent (see L. XLVIII *a*) and is repeated here.]

[2] Mason, *Works*, Ode viii, *On the Fate of Tyranny*, pp. 45–50.

131   9-2

fell into his Hands, wch after reading it, he told me he was vastly disappointed, for he had never redde any thing that gave him fewer Ideas, or less information. This led me to look it over, for the Original I had never seen since I was a Boy at Cambridge. I found the version to be in a clear good English Style, & aſsented fully to his Opinion. Some time ago I got Mr Alderson,[3] who was once My Curate, to cut Isaiah out of an old Bible, to interleave it, & to insert all the Passages that he thought cleard up any difficulty; his Copy I have revised, and it is surprising to see how little of consequence occurs, except what is contained in a mere change of Persons & Tenses. Dixon has promised me to do the same thing with Blaney's Version of Jeremiah, & I dare say it will turn out equally unimportant. Now all these three are endued with a full share of plain good Common Sense & Learning sufficient for such a task, therefore I would take their word before all the Westminsters & Etonians in the world, The Dean of Christ Church,[4] nay even My own Archbishop[5] not excepted.

I cannot possibly mend my Epitaph, & I verily think Your Lordship is in this case, as I have found you in some others, so fond of chastity in Composition, that it amounts even to Prudishneſs. the little turn or point, or whatever it may be called, wch it has, will certainly make it the better relished by the many, who in such case ought to be humourd. Even my own opinion is

[3] Christopher Alderson. See Introduction, p. xviii, n. 3.
[4] Cyril Jackson; he had succeeded Hurd as Preacher of Lincoln's Inn.
[5] William Markham, educated at Westminster and afterwards Headmaster when Jackson was his pupil.

that an Epitaph should be something like an Epigram, without a sting. And that brevity, wch is efsential to it, often produces this effect even when the Author did not intend it, wch in the present was precisely my case. But I will not tire your Lordship longer with my defence of it. I release you to the criticism on my two Birthday Sonnets[6] upon wch you have my full leave to exercise all your strictural powers, & like mitred Rochester *nod* your head[7] or not just as pleases you.

My kind Compliments attend your Nephew.

Believe me my Dear Lord

Yours devotedly & affectionately

W. MASON

Dixon left me the morning he rec^d your Letter. He is gone to Town about his Inclosure at Tuddington[8] by wch his living will be much encreas'd.

[6] The third side of his quarto paper is occupied by the two seventy-first birthday sonnets (*Works*, I, pp. 130, 129, sonnets IX and VIII), "Sonnet Prefatory" and "Sonnet Anniversary". In the versions, as published, there are verbal changes from those sent in the letter.

[7] [See Pope, *Epistle to Dr Arbuthnot*, l. 140:
"Ev'n mitred Rochester would nod the head".
In his "Sonnet Prefatory" Mason adapted the quotation to Hurd:
For Hurd, the critic of my youthful lay
And now Right Reverend Censor, crys 'Forbear;
Tis not for Age or Infancy to play
With pointed Tools; a Sonnet once a year
Or so, my Nod permits thee to efsay'.
Duteous I bow yet think the Doom severe.]

[8] John Dixon, Rector of Boughton, Northants, was also Rector of Toddington, Beds.

L

MASON *to* Hurd

Aston June 18th 1796

My dear Lord

I have just now heard that you have been upon your
Visitations[1] therefore, I hope, this will find you return'd in good health to quiet & Hartlebury, in w^ch
I hope too I may venture to send you under another
Cover, a private Copy of something I have lately
written,[2] to wch if you give your Episcopal & critical
Nod[3] it will flatter me extreamly. The types of it are
at York, not yet broke up, & this, the only corrected
proof I have yet received. my meaning is (if it paſses
your Lordship's *ordeal*) to take off only about half a
dozen copies more, that I may communicate them to
a few other friends.[4] were I to commit it again to the
Preſs, you will see, it should be done in a larger form &
with a number of Scriptural texts & illustrations of w^ch
I have by me already a considerable quantity, & in w^ch
perhaps Dr Burgh might aſsist me; but he, as yet, has
not seen any Part of what I now send you.

I know your Lordship is so much more inclin'd to
Pope's Manner than Dryden's that you will be likely
to blame me for not following the former. But in this

---

[1] Hurd, *Some Occurrences in my own Life*: "In the Summer of
1796 visited my Diocese in Person; I have great reason to suppose
for the last time; being in the 77th year of my age—*fiat voluntas
Dei!*" [He did so again in 1800, but in 1803 his visit was by
Commission.]   [2] His *Religio Clerici*, see n. 7.
[3] See L. XLIX, n. 7.
[4] Anna Seward wrote on 31 June 1796: "I learn with regret
that Mr Mason is going to print a new work of his by a private
press, for his friends only". *Letters of Anna Seward*, IV, p. 229.

134

case I think there was peculiar propriety in imitating the latter, wch I have done, even in his breach of Couplets, his Alexandrines, and even his triplets. Therefore I must beg you, if you favour me with your remarks, to adhere to the canon of Criticism, as much as pofsible, that I have laid down at Verse 216 P: 2^d to Verse 223, except you find some grammatical or other similar Errors.[5]

I have divided my Poem into two Parts, because the Creed itself, of wch I mean it to be a metrical exposition, consists I think of two different subjects: one the Trinity in Unity, the other the Incarnate Deity. and this Division, I think, will make the whole better understood.

But I will say no more on the matter, except concluding with a hope, that tho' I have broke my word with your Lordship, wch I gave you in my last Sonnet, & that in the same year in which I made the promise,[6] you will forgive me for so doing, whether you approve of what I have done or not, & as I made Spenser say half a century ago you will—

> rede aright, & if this *Christian* lay
> Thou nathless judgeth all too slight & vain,
> Let my *well-meaning* mend my *ill efsay*.—Musæus.

As the types are set I must beg your Lordship to return this single copy[7] as soon as pofsible, & then if I order

---

[5] Mason, *Works*, I, p. 447:
> "And now, my friend, if thy severest eye
> An error in my Christian creed descry;
> An error but in substance, not in style,
> I pray thee use thy hatchet, not thy file,
> And hew it down".

[6] See L. XLIX, n. 7.

[7] It is clear from Mason's next letter that Hurd returned "this single copy" with his criticisms and that Mason rectified most of

more than a single one to be taken off for myself, I shall send you another. With my kind Compliments to your Nephew

I am, my Dear Lord, with true respect &c

Yours most cordially

W. MASON

In these times, if this proves any amusement to you, it will turn your thoughts, not only from the Continental Storms,[8] but those much nearer & more alarming, that blow from Carlton House.[9] I am a perfect convert to your Lordship's Hypothesis of Insanity.

the passages to which Hurd objected. He then had a dozen copies printed and one of these he sent to Hurd: this, no doubt, is the copy that remains in the fold of Mason's letter. The title is not printed but Mason had written the heading "Religio Clerici or the Faith of a Clergyman of the Church of England written in Imitation of Mᵣ Dryden's Religio Laici", followed by the quotation from Jude iii in Greek.

In Part I, ll. 135, 137 (of the poem as published) "Lindsey" (see L. LI, n. 3), and in Part II, l. 20 "Paine Knight M P", have been written to fill blanks in the text.

On the back of the proof copy Hurd had noted some suggested changes. He would prefer to read "quirks" for "rules" in Part I, l. 13; "hewn" for "dash'd" in l. 63; "how far" for "wherefore" in l. 172. Mason did not adopt any of these. He did, however, accept Hurd's advice that in l. 100

"In Liberal Metre, not in labour'd Lays"

it was better to substitute "careless" for "liberal". Possibly these notes were kept for proposal to Mason *viva voce* when he paid his usual visit to Hartlebury that autumn. Mason made many other alterations in the poem before it reached the form in which it was published.

[8] Bonaparte's campaign against Austria in Italy had lately begun.

[9] [A final separation between the Prince and the Princess of Wales had recently taken place.]

LI

MASON *to* Hurd

Aston July 9th 96

My dear Lord,

I am sorry the proof of my R. C. came to your Lordship so inopportunely but am therefore the more obliged to you for examining it & transmitting it to me again so speedily. After having rec^d your imprimatur, I employd a morning in rectifying most of the Pafsages you had so justly objected to, some lines seem'd to me not to have appeard clear to you from false punctuation only, others from perhaps your not knowing to what I precisely alluded therefore these latter I sufferd to remain. I then sent my Alterations to York and orderd my Printer (who I can safely confide in) to take off a dozen copies, very few of wch I shall at present communicate to any person besides your Lordship to whom I now send one under a separate cover.[1]

The notes many of wch are now written are not merely textual, nor are they intended to load the page. But (should ever the Poem be made publici juris)[2] are illustrative & to be placed at the End. Notes of this kind I think will be useful if not even absolutely necefsary to such Readers as I have said I write for, and as I shall treat certain Socinian arguments[3] in them as *detected Falshoods* I shall venture to make them a *butt for Wit*; some of Lindsey's[4] particularly, who has

[1] See L. L, n. 7.
[2] *Religio Clerici* was not published till 1811 (Mason, *Works*, I, p. 427), with Annotations illustrative and critical on p. 451.
[3] Theophilus Lindsey, the Unitarian, had been Mason's contemporary at St John's. [4] E.g. on Lindsey, ll. 454, 456.

137

much offended me by his dull pertnefs respecting your Lordship in a preface wch he lately writ to usher in some trash of Priestley's imported from America, & wch I take for granted you never saw.

I will not be hasty in expecting a further Critique from you, tho I shall wish to know that the Pacquet is rec'd safe. For as I mean to make you a visit this summer (when Summer is actually set in, wch with us is not yet the case) I shall wait for your further strictures vivâ voce.

Believe me My Dear Lord,

Yours most respectfully & cordially

W. MASON

My kind Compt^s to your Nephew. I hear poor Main-waring is, or has been dangerously ill at Stratton.[5]

---

[5] John Mainwaring, a friend of Mason and Hurd, often mentioned in this correspondence, was born at Drayton Bassett, Staffs., and graduated from St John's College in 1745, which was also Mason's year. He was elected to a fellowship at St John's, and was appointed by Lord Weymouth to the benefice of Church Stretton (he also held that of Aberdaron in Carnarvonshire), and it is at this "Stratton" that Mason hears of him as being ill. He was chosen Lady Margaret Professor of Divinity at Cambridge in 1788, and died in April 1807 (*The Gentleman's Magazine*, April 1807, p. 386). His sermons were published in 1780 and Hurd bought a copy. There is prefixed to them an interesting dissertation with notes, and the final note (xcvii) takes us with him right into the circle. He is dealing with "the *fatal jealousy of Authorship*"; witness Pope and Addison. But, says he, "it is more satisfactory to conclude these Notes with a striking instance of the contrary kind, and perfectly in point. For the late Mr Gray, and his illustrious friend not only excelled greatly as Poets; but precisely in the same species of Poetry;—a circumstance, which, instead of impairing the early affection that subsisted between them, served only to strengthen and cement it". Mason must have delighted in that tribute.

LII

MASON *to* Hurd

Aston Oct. 3ᵈ 1796

My dear Lord,

I arrived safe here[1] in good time to receive my Arch-
diaconal Visitation, and to receive also due applause
for the good condition in wᶜʰ he[2] found my Church
Parsonage &c. His Father he tells me is in good
health, and either gone or about to go to Town. I hope
this Letter also will find Your Lordship freed from the
incipient attack wᶜʰ threatened you & shall be glad
to hear that you are so.

The rumbling of my Chaise wheels, like those of
Sir R. Blackmore's chariot,[3] brought into my mind
the following mode of finishing the Epitaph. be
pleasd to tell me if the lines *arride* you more than
the former.

> Witnefs those numerous Years of ceaseless Pain,
> Wᶜʰ Christian Patience arm'd her to sustain,
> And heav'nly Hope that, hov'ring o'er her head,
> The brilliant Palm of bliss Eternal spread.[4]

[1] The promised summer visit to Hartlebury (see L. LI) had
been paid.
[2] Robert Markham, the Archbishop's son; King's Sch., Westminster, 1782; Archdeacon of the West Riding, 1794–1837; also
Rector of Bolton Percy, Yorks.
[3] Sir Richard Blackmore, physician to William III and Queen
Anne, produced in 1695 in folio *Prince Arthur, an Heroick Poem in
X Books*, about which he said in his preface that it had been written
during the odd moments of a busy practice in coffee-houses or
elsewhere, "or in passing up and down the streets" in the chariot
to which Mason refers.
[4] [See L. XLVII, n. 7, L. XLVIII, n. 9. Mason had, no doubt,
discussed the epitaph on his visit to Hurd.]

Believe me to be with all kind Compliments to your Nephew

My dear Lord

Yours most truly & respectfully

W. MASON

I have rec^d all my Letters safe but sorry you have had the trouble of so much franking.

LIII

MASON *to* Hurd

Aston Oct. 12th 1796

My dear Lord,

The same day that I rec^d the pleasure of your Lordship's letter wch gave me an acc^t of your amendment from your late attack from the Gout & also your *fiat* to my couplet (wch should I find myself necefsitated to make the rest of the lines public shall now be adopted) I also receivd in a pacquet from York The Letter to Lord Sheffield[1] wch I have redde twice over, & very highly approve. It ought I think to be an added exception to your favorite axiom "that the age of Five & forty ought to be the term when our literary efforts should cease". For here is another Septuagenarian, who writes with as much spirit & correctnefs

---

[1] *A Letter to the Right Honourable John Lord Sheffield, on the Publication of the Memoirs and Letters of the late Edward Gibbon Esq.* had just been published. The author was Professor Mainwaring.

as he did in what your Lordship would deem the Acme of his faculties. You find by all this that I agree with your supposition as to the Author,[2] &, if he be now with you, I beg you will tell him that the pleasure I have rec'd from his Pamphlet, great as it is, is only secondary to that which I feel from learning that his health is so much þetter than, from report, I had reason to think. & that my late Epistolary silence was purely occasioned by the fear of distreſsing his Eyes by inducing him to read my scrawl.—on a similar acc.ᵗ the smallneſs of the type in wᶜʰ for œconomy I printed the private copy of my Rel: Cler: prevents me from requesting him, if still with you, to read it & favour me with his opinion of it—I have now altered my Chemical lines[3] in it, so as to make them Orthodoxly Lavoiserian, in wᶜʰ I have been assisted by Mᵣ Gisborne[4] who is more versed in these matters than I am, & I shall put them on the next page that you may insert them on

---

[2] Hurd's copy of the *Letter* is marked "by J. M. Prof. of Div. [L. M.] Camb." The Bishop went through it and corrected some misprints, and had it bound with three of Mainwaring's sermons and nine of Bishop Hallifax. The *Letter* contains on p. 43 a reference to Hurd, which had speedy consequences. "Nothing", it says, "can be more admirable than the address of Dᵣ Hurd (now Bishop of Worcester) in his answer to the letter of Mᵣ G. concerning the authenticity of the book of Daniel ... The Letter [i.e Gibbon's] is not inserted [in Lord Sheffield's Memoirs], and perhaps a copy of it was not taken or preserved. However, the substance of it is seen in the Answer [i.e. Hurd's], which is of considerable length, and which stamps a value on the whole collection." Mainwaring's *Letter* is dated 1 July 1796. On Nov. 18 of that year Hurd dated at Hartlebury Castle the Appendix to his Sermons on the Prophecies (1772), in which he included Gibbon's letter as well as his own answer, "after the secret had been kept for twice twelve years" (*Works* (1811), v, pp. 363 ff.).
[3] *Religio Clerici*, Mason, *Works*, i, p. 436, ll. 244–51.
[4] Rev. Thomas Gisborne; see above, L. XLII, n. 5.

141

the blank page of your Copy if you think it worth while.[5] Your Lordship will laugh at my Gnomes and Sylphs. But this species of absurd Personification is as much in D͏ͬ Darwin's manner as the general run of my Poem is in Dryden's, & will so be thought by Readers more versed in the Loves of the Plants than I suspect your Lordship to be.

The Archdeacon has been so obliging as to offer to appear for me at the Minster the few Sundays remaining of my residence (and Sunday is now on acc͏ͭ of the repairs the only day on w͏ᶜʰ Service is redde) but as he cannot return to York till the 19͏ᵗʰ I believe I shall go thither next Saturday & thence pay a visit in that Neighbourhood but shall return to Aston as soon as pofsible.

With kind Compliments to the Profefsor, if with you, & your Nephew I remain my good Lord

Yours most cordially

W. MASON

I think the Pamphlet[6] treats the noble Editor more civilly than I should have done, or expected others would have done by me if I had added to my Memoirs of Gray his common place book, worth however a million of Gibbons.

[On the third page of his letter Mason had written his new version and a note.]

---

[5] Hurd thought it worth while to strike out the discarded lines and substitute these in their right place.
[6] See n. 1.

Part 1st

Dele Lines 246, 247, 248, 249, & insert the following[7]:

He knows two Gnomes, who spring from mine or mote,
In gallic greek call'd Carbone & Azote,
By secret spells allure to their embrace
Bright Oxigen, a Sylph of heavnly race,
And from their union close of filth & fire
Produce that Atmosphere we both respire,
W^{ch}, did they not, he could not screw his Lyre
To that high pitch etc.

NOTE

According to Lavoisier, *Oxigen* is what former Chemists called dephlogisticated or vital air. *Azote* what they termed Phlogiston $< \cdot >$ and to what they entitled mephitic or fixed air, He gives the name of *Carbone*. These two latter airs are both of them destructive of Life & flame, but, with the former in combination, constitute Atmospheric Air. *Carbone* is the heaviest of the three, and *Hydrogen*, wch is still lighter, & like *Oxigen* inflamable, composes with that Water.

---

[7] In Part 1 of *Religio Clerici* Mason was combining the ideas of Erasmus Darwin and Lavoisier in a kind of chemical justification of the Trinity, and his lines as first printed ran thus:

> He knows that Oxygen and Hydrogen
> (Words fitter for a Greek than English pen)
> Their separate powers and properties combine,
> And, with Azote, compose by mixture trine
> That atmospheric air, we both respire,
> Which, if destroy'd, he could not screw his Lyre....

In the final version there was a slight modification of the last three lines, which were as follows:

> Mix with her purity their filth and fire
> To form that atmosphere we both respire,
> Which did they not, nor he could screw his Lyre....

143

LIV
MASON *to* Hurd

My dear Lord

[*January 1797*][1]

You will find by the next page that I go scribbling on to the end of the Chapter. But you must forgive me, it is my principal Amusement. The 28 Chapter of Job appears to me to be quite a *purpureus pannus* totally unconnected with all of Job's final defence, w either went before or follows it. Yet, when considered in this detatchd Light, it also appears to be a Complete Ode, & of the very first & most perfect Lyrical form when somewhat clear'd from its oriental redundancies, w in my Version is here done. Our Bible Version of this Chapter is peculiarly obscure &, I suspect, Faulty. Yet if, according to a conjecture of Albert Schultens,[2] we insert in the beginning of the third verse *Man for he,* much of the obscurity will be removed. Schultens however had no idea that it was a Lyrical composition, for he only calls it Peroratio magnifica pro Coronide imposita universis disputationibus, w it is so far from being, that Job continues his speech in the very next Chapter, taking up a quite different subject, a narrative of his former state of prosperity. But all this is of that species of Lauda Bene Criticism, w men, conversant with words more than sentiments, must necefsarily make, & if they are able to exprefs themselves in what is called Clafsical Latinity they will obtain that degree of celebrity, w the Lecturer of Job got, who, I dare say, never knew the merit of this peculiar

[1] The letter is not dated, but Hurd replied (L. LV) on 24 January 1797.
[2] [Albert Schultens (1688–1750), Professor of Oriental Languages at Leyden.]

Chapter w^ch, had he known it, & in consequence versified it in Alcaics or otherwise, He would have done more than he has done by his Versions of what all the world before knew were either pathetic or sublime.

What I wish from your Lordship is merely this, that you would note what you think requires emendation in this Copy, provided you think it deserves such pains, & if you do, I mean to print it in a private way, with a short address to you, explanatory, like this Letter of the Idea I have conceivd of the Original. I shall put down a few references at the Bottom of this page to Lefsen your trouble.

My third Volume³ I find is publish'd, & the Book-sellers to whom the 500 Copies were sold, have put a Lying Advertisement to it, viz. that the Book consists *wholly* of things not before published. But the Best of Booksellers (& I believe they who have it are the best) are what our good Bp W. would have called *Scounderels*. I have not yet heard a syllable about it from any of my Correspondents.

I wish your Lordship & Nephew all good and seasonable wishes, hoping that your health has not been affected by the hitherto severe winter. Believe me to be with all sincerity

Your Lordship's truely respectful Serv.ᵗ
W. MASON

³ [Mason was publishing a new edition of his poems, of which vols. I and II appeared in 1796. A prefatory note to the third volume explained that it contained with "a few occasional Odes, etc., before published separately, such (poems) as have stolen into the world surreptitiously and others (chiefly juvenile compositions) that rested in MS..in the hands of different persons". The title-page described the book as "Poems by William Mason, M.A., Vol. III, Now first published". To this description Mason objected.]

Reference.

First Strophe includes the text of the first
6 Bible verses.

1 Antistrophe from the 6 to about the 11th.
2 Epode   the single 12th verse.
2   from the 12th to the 24 V: but here
              Schultens rather than the old Version,
              is often followd, particularly that of
              the sculpturd Vase is from him. And
              the imagery of Celestial intelligencies
              instead of what the Bible calls the fowls
              of the air. I suspect Death & Destruc-
              tion come from the same *root* with *Chaos*
              or *Void*, and I have given my Version
              that cast.
2^d Antistrophe from the 24th to the last but one.
              Follows Schultens much more than the
              Bible Version.
3^d Epode   wch only paraphrases the moral of the
              Whole Ode.⁴

⁴ The *Ode on Wisdom taken from Job Chap. 28th*, neatly transcribed
by the curate, occupies the rest of the paper. In nearly a dozen
lines there are differences from the version printed in 1811
(*Works*, 1, pp. 87 ff.), showing that the poet was never content, or
resulting, perhaps, from the Bishop's suggestions, though at first
he found nothing to alter: e.g. in 1, 1, l. 6 "their darkling vigils"
became "their useless vigils"; in l. 9 "hid Treasures" became
"bright sapphires"; and in 1, 2, l. 7 the short line
    "But did this all-pervading Man"
was lengthened into
    "But did this bold, this all-pervading Man".

146

LV

HURD *to* Mason

H.C. Jan. 24, 1797

Dear Sir

I have your Letter without date, & your *Ode on Wisdom*. You have picked some gold out of Schultens dunghill.[1] But these dull interpreters are not much worth your notice. You may venture without scruple on *man* for *he*. Houbigant[2] translates v. 3 thus—Nihil jam tenebris opertum; nihil rarum et pretiosum. Reperit *homo* gemmas abditissimas—and in a note, *ille* est homo, de quo in fine capitis superioris. v. 19. You may make use of Schultens' *vase*,[3] tho' Houbigant translates, as our bible does,—*auro non compensabitur defæcato*—v. 21 *celestial intelligences* seems nobler than *the fowls of the air*. But I doubt it's truth. The former may be supposed to know that *obedience* is true wisdom; not so, blind mortals, or even the eagle-eyed inhabitants of air. Houbigant's version is, Ea [Sapientia] mortalium omnium latet aspectibus; ea cœli volucribus abscondita. But the authority of Schultens will justify you, if you prefer his comment. And now to your questions. I not only approve your Ode but think it excellent. Nor do I find a single verse, or word to alter.

As soon as I saw your new volume advertized, I ordered our Worcester bookseller to send for it. But

[1] Albert Schultens, *Liber Jobi*. Hurd had the 1737 edition in two volumes.
[2] C. F. Houbigant, *Biblia Hebraica*, 4 vols. Paris, 1753, III, pp. 193, 194, n. 3.
[3] Schultens, *op. cit.* p. 782: "aut permutatio ejus vas aureum".

147   10-2

it is not yet arrived.[4]—Our booksellers are grown rich & great, & therefore inattentive. I don't wonder they blundered in the advertisement; if it be a blunder, for it makes for them, tho' not for the author.

Your report of Roscoe's[5] book made me send for it. He seems well versed in the Tuscan history & literature. He, also, writes an easier style (tho' not without affectation) & is more decent than Gibbon. But he is of that school in religion, & in politics, a Jacobin. So fine a thing it seems to our modern historians & Virtuosi to have, & to profess to have, no religion.[6]

I scribble this in haste on that day, on wch I enter by God's great mercy on my 78th year. Yet here I am, reading and criticizing your poetry. But it is divine poetry, & not unworthy it's subject. May you live long to amuse yourself in this way, & to oblige & entertain your old friend & affectionate servant

R. WORCESTER

P.S. My nephew is much your's. If anything more occurs to me on the subject of your Ode, you shall hear again from me.

[4] It arrived and is still at Hartlebury.
[5] The Bishop bought the second edition of William Roscoe, *Life of Lorenzo de' Medici,* 2 vols, 1796, and discussed it in his *Commonplace Book,* III, p. 131, using many of the phrases which occur in this letter to Mason.
[6] [Kilvert, p. 251, prints a verse from Hurd's *Commonplace Book:*

On some late Historians.

Teach me, Historic Muse, to mix
Impiety with politics,
So shall I write, *nil aliud posco,*
Like my lov'd Gibbon, Hume, and Roscoe.]

LVI

Mason *to* Hurd

Aston Jan: 31ˢᵗ 1797

My dear Lord,

I am highly gratified by the Approbation you have given to me of my Ode. I own I rather thought well of it myself, but I writ it with so much greater facility than I did that from Isaiah[1] forty years ago, that I suspected I had only acquired by habit a quickness of execution, but might have lost a strength of colouring and expression.

I am afraid Scultens, of whom I have as mean an opinion as your Lordship, will not either authorize the Sculptured Vase or the Cœlestial Intelligences. the Truth is, I took them from a French Version of Schultens translated by Messʳˢ Joncourt Sacretaire & Allemand printed at Leiden 1748 The latter of whom Allemand came over with the Dutch Ambaſsador on the King's Acceſsion &, on seeing me at Lord Holdernefse's, sent it me when he returnd. This version is said in the preface to have been revised & approved by Schultens himself. But on consulting his wretched Latin in Dʳ R Gray's edition (the only Hebrew Book in my Poſseſsion) I find no Authority for either of the Paſsages, one of which according to Schultens[2] is

    17. Non certabit ei aurum & crystallus pellucida
        Aut permutatio ejus vas aureum.

---

[1] [*Ode on the Fate of Tyranny*, described as "a free paraphrase of the 14ᵗʰ Chapter of Isaiah". *Works*, I, p. 45.]
[2] Schultens, *op. cit.* pp. 782, 786.

149

The other

21. Et enim obsignata est ab omni vivente
Et a volucre cœlorum est occultata.

But I will keep the thing by me a little while, & then make the Lines in question more *germane* to the Hebrew Verity.

Houbigant, for the extracts from whom I am much obliged to Your Lordship, is, I fancy an Hebraist of a better form, but how strange it is that one Word can mean either *flame* or *Bread*?

I cannot however see the Connection, wch your Lordship calls so close, in the Original. You must know, that ten or twelve years ago I versified the whole Poetical part of Job into dramatic Verse.[3] But it appear'd Prolix, & I threw it aside. This Winter I happen'd to find it amongst other Ebauchées, and have since returnd it to the anvill, versified the Prose Introduction & conclusion, so that it appears a sort of Epo-dramatic Composition similar as to manner with Paradise Regained. I give your Lordship this information merely to add that this Chapter puzzled me so much, that I could not pofsibly connect it with what preceeded it. I found it so perfectly Lyrical, & breaking off so abruptly, therefore I versified it in unequal Couplets of two tens & two eights like Milton's version of Quis multa Gracilis &c,[4] but as I knew you did not like Blank Verse (neither do I the unequal Blank Verse) I try'd my hand at it again in Strophe &c

[3] Mason told Lord Harcourt in 1789: "I am versifying the Book of Job" (*Harcourt Papers*, VII, p. 154; Draper, *Mason*, p. 100).
[4] The translation of Horace, *Odes*, I, 5: "What slender youth bedew'd with liquid odours", etc.

Rhymed, in the way in wch I sent it for Your Lordship's amusement. As to Houbigant's Dictum that it refers to *Men* in the last verse of the preceding Chapter, My Bible prints the word in *Italics*, wch indicates it not to be in the original, so this necessary word is omitted in each place.[5]

For myself I am not displeasd with the Pains I have taken with the whole Book, as I think it has given me a clearer insight into what you call this Mysterious Composition, & convinced me that Our friend's[6] Conjecture, tho' certainly only a conjecture, is the best & only clue to direct one thro' the Labyrinth.

Believe me to be,
My Dear Lord
Your obligd & affectionate Servt
W. MASON

LVII

MASON *to* Hurd

Aston March 4th 97

My dear Lord,

I have rec^d your Lordship's obliging Letter with the proof inclosed, wch I shall immediately return to my Printer with the addrefs[1] wch you suffer me to have the honour of prefixing to it. You know me well enough to think that I shall not omit the part of it wch I like best, having your Licence for the same. But I

---

[5] Mason was not a Hebraist, and indeed disliked such people.
[6] Bp. Warburton [H].
[1] [*An Address to the Right Reverend the Bishop of Worcester* was prefixed to the Ode.]

wish your Lordship had returned the MS.,[2] for I retained only an imperfect first Draught, from wch I have been obliged to transcribe another for the Printer, wch I fear will be less correct. Therefore I must beg you to send it to me by the first post, that I may compare & correct the first *paged* Proof of the whole, wch I hope to have in the course of next week.

I forgot to ask you in my last whether Old Sam Westley's Comment on Job is not in your Library.[3] I suspect it is, because I know Mr Pope patronized the poor Old Tory (see His Letter to Swift 45 vol. 9).[4] I saw the Book once, with Pope's name in the list of subscribers, but merely saw it; 'tis a well printed Folio in Latin. Now as this said Westley had more of the Poet about him than most Hebraists, either before or after him, I think he is more likely to have discoverd the Lyrical cast of the 28th chap. than any body else. For my Part, he ranks with me, as an *Epic* Poet, full as high as your favorite Cowley does, & would certainly have excelld him, had it not unfortunately been the fashion of the time to imitate him, wch Wesley, then a very young Man in a state of Penury &, I believe, a Lincolnshire fen curate, thought the best road to celebrity. I have heard Dr Warburton speak of his notes to his Life of Christ with approbation, & they are certainly both Learned & oddly entertaining.

[2] I.e. of the Address.
[3] In 1735, when Wesley's Dissertation was subscribed for, Hurd was fifteen. Mason probably expects that Pope's copy passed to Warburton and so was acquired by Hurd. But what Hurd bought was the Warburton collection at the Gloucester palace. The rest of Warburton's books were in Grosvenor Square.
[4] See above, L. XXXIX, n. 6.

I send your Lordship my third Anniversary Sonnet[5] at the joint request of you and your Nephew, to whom my kind compliments. after making candid Allowance on acc.ᵗ of the Lapse of another year, I hope, you will not think it much inferior to those, wᶜʰ preceeded it. Your Lordship will perceive that I make my ability to compose a metrical Confeſsion of my Faith in the R.L.,[6] the work of the past year, the concluding theme of my gratitude. *I have a sharp & sorry Rheum offends me,*[7] viz. a cold in my Head that makes my Transcription of it troublesome. Therefore I hope you will be content to read it in a better hand.

Believe me, to be, My Dear Lord,

Very cordially yours

W. MASON

I fear those worst of Savages the French send their Vagabonds, Galley slaves &c. over for the purpose of loading us with Prisoners; wᶜʰ, to guard, will do harm to our National Defence. I should not wonder to hear of more sent over for this diabolical purpose.

---

[5] Sonnet x, *February 23, 1797 Anniversary (Works*, I, p. 131), transcribed in the same hand as the *Ode on Wisdom* (see L. LIV, n. 4), was enclosed. The Bishop with his own hand corrected the copy in accordance with Mason's next letter, and the text as corrected is identical with the printed version, except that in l. 7 "Spring's impatient heralds" was altered to "Spring's impartial heralds".

[6] The writer is muddled between *Religio Laici* and *Religio Clerici.*

[7] [Shakespeare, *Othello,* III, iv, 48.]

LVIII

MASON *to* Hurd

Aston March 20th 1797

My dear Lord,

You have with this the Ode[1] fresh from the Prefs w^ch,
I hope, you will find correctly printed. I have only
taken off a single Dozen Copies, but if you wish for any
more of them to give to particular friends, your Lordship has only to write for them. I do not think I shall
give away above half the number. But I mean to send
to my Lord of London, who, I hope, will show it[2] to
my Lord of Durham who is the present Patron, to
whom the Hebraists pay their court. One of these (as
I see in the British Critic) has lately published a new
Translation of the Book of Job, & the Editors have
selected as a specimen part of this very 28th Chap: a
Version wch for English, out does Scultens Latin.
Mercy on us! What will become of our Bible, if they
go on at this rate!

With kind compliments to your Nephew I remain

My Dear Lord

Yours with all respect and affection

W. MASON

[1] The *Ode on Wisdom, A Private Copy*, its leaves not opened, is
still with the letter.

[2] Mason also sent Bishop Porteus his Anniversary sonnet.
Hannah More relates that "The Bishop of London was just
reading us a sonnet he (Mason) had sent him on his seventy-
second birthday, when the account of his death came" (Roberts,
Hannah More, II, p. 14, quoted by Draper, *Mason*, p. 119).

Corrigenda in the Sonnet.

And still (thank Heaven) if I not falsely deem,
My Lyre, yet vocal, freely can afford
Strains not discordant.[3]

LIX

MASON *to* Hurd

Aston Ap. 3 —*97*

My dear Lord,

I inclose, as you desire, another Copy of the Ode.
My Curate who is at once my Orthographer &
Punctuator, vindicates himself from your Lordship's
criticisms by saying that the distinction between E're
& Eer is now little regarded, but I kifs the rod; there
is certainly too many *eers*[1] of one sort or other in the
Ode, as it now stands, but at present it can't be helpt.

I am a little, tho' not much, curious to know whether
His Grace of Grafton[2] has made a present to Your
Lordship & consequently to Hartlebury Library of
a New Edition of Profefsor Greisbatch[3] first Vol: of
his Greek Testament. I have had that inexprefsible
Honour. If you have not, you will perhaps smile to
know that this Celsifsimus Dux bonarum Literarum
patronus Egregius has had a certain number of Copies

---

[3] The original version (see L. LVII, n. 5) had for these lines:
"And (thanks to Heav'n) if I not falsely deem,
My Lyre, as yet unstrung, can still afford
Notes not discordant &c.".

[1] "Ere" occurs five times in the Ode, twice in the sense of *ever*,
three times in that of *before*.
[2] Augustus Henry Fitzroy, third Duke, Chancellor of the University of Cambridge.
[3] Hurd's only Griesbach was the edition of 1776, 1777 (Halle).

155

printed at Halle in Saxony on fine *English* paper, wch he makes presents of, & for wch the Learned Profefsor gives him due Encomiums in his *Prefatio.* With kind comp^{ts} to your Nephew I remain My Dear Lord

Yours most truely

W. MASON

(Note in the Bishop's handwriting:

This was the last Letter I received from my old and much esteemed friend. He dyed two days after (Apr. 5th) in consequence of a slight accident, mentioned in the annexed Letter of the same day from his Curate.[4]

R. W.)

[4] See Appendix A, L. I*.

APPENDIX A

I*

THE REV. M. BRUNSKILL *to the*
Bishop of Worcester

Aston Apl 5. 1797

My Lord,

I am very sorry to trouble your Lordship on so melancholy an occasion. On Friday last Mr Mason received a slight scratch upon his Leg, from which he felt no inconvenience till Monday Morning,[1] when he complained of pain, & in the Evening had an aguish fit. On Tuesday afternoon, notwithstanding the best medical afsistance that could be had, there were appearances of a mortification; a Stupor ensued, & he pafsed a restlefs night, & he expired on this day[2] about two o'Clock in the afternoon.

I am, My Lord,

With all due respect

Your obdt & humble Servt

M. BRUNSKILL[3] (Curate)

[1] On this Monday he wrote his last letter to the Bishop (L. LIX) but gave him no hint of his accident.

[2] Mason's monument in Westminster Abbey gives April 7 as the date of his death. This letter shows that the date is wrong and that he died on April 5.

[3] Mason's curate at Aston, to whom he left a legacy.

II*

The Bishop of Worcester *to* Mr Montagu[1]
[Copy][2]

Hartlebury Castle Aug. 10 1799

Dear Sir,

I have your favour of the 3ᵈ, with Mʳ Stonhewer's obliging Letter;[3] I wonder you did not immediately let him know, as you honestly might, that my *old* head[4] is unequal to the task of composing an epitaph for Mʳ Mason. But, in remembrance of our friendship, I shall make an effort to explain at least the notion that I have of such a thing.

In the first place, I am no friend to Epitaphs in *verse*, no not to that of our friend himself on Mʳ Gray.[5]

[1] Frederick Montagu, of Papplewick, Nottinghamshire, whose mother was one of Mason's dowagers (see L. XXXII, n. 4), M.P. from 1759 to 1790, was a friend of Gray and Mason. When Mason was appointed Residentiary Canon at York, Gray wrote: "he owes it to our friend Mʳ F: Montagu, who is Brother-in-Law to Dean Fountayne". (Tovey, II, p. 248.) Frederick Montagu died at Papplewick on 30 July 1800.

[2] The copy is in the hand of Richard Hurd, junior.

[3] [The Bishop's letter is explained by an unpublished letter of Stonhewer to Christopher Alderson of August 20, 1799. Stonhewer and Hurd were carrying on an indirect correspondence, with Montagu as intermediary. The monument which Stonhewer and Alderson were intending to erect in Westminster Abbey to Mason's memory was all but finished, and the epitaph had to be considered. Montagu had recently been at Hartlebury, when the Bishop had expressed to him his "opinion as to the kind of epitaph he should approve". Stonhewer, on hearing this from Montagu, had written that he "not only lik'd the Bishop's Idea, but wish'd to see it executed by himself". This letter Montagu had sent to the Bishop, and the letter printed here is the Bishop's reply, containing his suggestion for an epitaph.]

[4] He was then in his 80th year.

[5] Mason, *Works*, I, p. 141: the four lines inscribed on the memorial to Gray in Westminster Abbey.

Let it be in *prose* then, but not *fine* prose; and I think for many reasons it should be in *Latin*.

In the next place, it is only in his character of *poet*, that this honour is to be done to our friend in Westminster Abbey. Let that then be the single subject of the epitaph, without enlarging on his other talents & qualities.

Lastly, that *one* subject should be touched in *language* simple, concise, and energetic.

If these premises are granted, what if something like the following be attempted—

Optimo Viro,

Gulielmo Mason, A. M.

Poetæ,

Si quis alius,

Culto, casto, pio

S.

Ob. Aprilis 5. 1797, æt. 72.[6]

When you write to M.r Stonhewer, you may suggest to him this idea, not of the epitaph to be adopted, but

[6] With the copy of the Bishop's letter is in his own script "Another form":

Optimum Virum

Gulielmum Mason;

Poetam

Verbis, numeris, sententiis

Felicem, varium, gravem

Immortalitati commendat

Hoc Marmor

Ob. etc.

[This must have been sent at a later date. In his letter of August 20 Stonhewer refers only to "the Epitaph", but in a letter to Alderson of November 14 he mentions the "Second Epitaph". By that time both forms had been submitted to the Bishop of London, who was strongly in favour of the first, as were Alderson and Stonhewer himself, and it was inscribed on the monument.]

of the turn & cast of it, only. You will also excuse to him my presumption in going thus far.

As to the Epitaph at *Aston*, that is another thing. It should be in English, may be considerably longer, & should descend to a detail of his preferments and qualifications.[7]

I have only to add that I am,

Dear Sir,

Your affectionate humble Servant

R. WORCESTER

P.S. I am glad your *Urns*[8] are in such forwardness. When they are finished, could not you contrive that I might have casts, or at least drawings of them?

[7] With the copy of the Bishop's letter, there is also in his own hand "A sketch of an Inscription on M.r M.'s monument at Aston":

Near this place
Lie the remains of William Mason M.A.
Præcentor and Residentiary of York,
And forty two years Rector of this Church.
He was endeared to his friends
By many virtues;
And to his parishioners,
in particular,
By his hospitality & charity.
He rebuilt his parsonage house,
And generally resided in it:
For, with the splendid talents
Which made him known in the world,
And had procured his preferment,
His ambition was to approve himself
A good parish priest
By a personal discharge of his pastoral duties.
He was born Feb. 12. 1725, O.S.,
And died April 5. 1797.

[The Bishop's nephew notes "Intended but not adopted".]
[8] To the memory of Mr Gray and Mr Mason [H]. [The urns mounted on square stone pedestals are still to be found on either bank of the River Leen, which flows through the grounds of

III*

The Rev. John Dixon[1] *to*
Richard Hurd, junior

Exmouth, Devon
Dec.r 9.th 1807

Dear Sir

I am sorry I did not see D.r Lucas[2] when I called upon him at Northampton the summer before last. When I called a second time, he was set out for Worcestershire. I was glad to hear from him by M.r Percival, & since from other quarters, a good account of the Bishop of Worcester's health. Had I seen D.r Lucas I intended to have sent a Message to you to be communicated to the Bishop relative to M.r Mason's works. D.r Burgh promised M.r Stonhewer and me

Papplewick Hall. On one pedestal there is an inscription: "To Thomas Gray" followed by six lines from his *Ode to Spring*, beginning "Beside some water's rushy Brink", with the initials F. M. below. The other pedestal is inscribed

"To William Mason,
Genio Loci.
Hail, sylvan wonders, hail and hail the hand
Whose native taste thy native charms display'd,
And taught one little acre to command
Each envied happiness of scene and shade.
F. M."

The quotation is from Mason's *Elegy Written in the Garden of a Friend, Works*, I, p. 102.]

[1] [The Rev. John Dixon, Rector of Boughton, Northants. (L. XLVI, n. 8), Christopher Alderson (see p. xviii above) and Richard Stonhewer (L. XLIII, n. 2), had been appointed Trustees of Mason's landed property, and they, in co-operation with Dr Burgh, were to be responsible for the publication of a complete edition of Mason's Works (see n. 3 below). The object of this letter is to explain the delay in publication.]

[2] Robert Lucas, D.D., Rector of Ripple, Worcs., and Vicar of Pattishall, Northants., married a niece of Bishop Hurd.

nine years ago in London to set about preparing an Edition of all Mr Mason's works already published with the sermons & such MSS as the Trustees should agree to publish.[3] We waited some time in expectation of seeing this promise fulfilled, but nothing was done. Five years ago I took a Journey into Yorkshire, my principal motive being to expedite this busine∫s. Accordingly Mr Alderson & I went to York to remind Dr Burgh of his promise, & to instigate him, if po∫sible, to set about this desirable work. He faithfully & repeatedly promised us to do so without further lo∫s of time. We were however soon convinced, that no dependance was to be placed on his promises. I went down into Yorkshire again two years & a half ago, & made a point of waiting on Dr Burgh at York. Mr Alderson did not then accompany me, having just received a letter from him, a∫suring him (Mr A.) as Dr Burgh then did me vivâ voce, that he would make

[3] A clause in Mason's will directed that Dr William Burgh, together with his three Trustees (see n. 1 above), were to select such unpublished manuscripts in Prose and Verse, that he might leave, which they should think proper for publication and that these should be printed with his writings already published in one complete edition, and that Dr Burgh should attend to the correct printing of the same, "for which friendly trouble" Mason desired him to accept "The Miniature Picture of Milton, painted by Cooper", which was bequeathed to him by Sir Joshua Reynolds.
[Dr Burgh, who had previously edited Mason's *English Garden*, accepted the task "as a duty imposed by Gratitude and Affection". From unpublished letters written by him and by Stonhewer to Christopher Alderson, as well as from this and a later letter of Dixon's, it is obvious that he altogether failed to discharge the duty. In September 1806 he had written to Alderson that he was "really now going to be occupied and to proceed without inter-mi∫sion". He had even ordered paper for an edition of a thousand copies. This letter of Dixon's shows that more than a year later he had made no progress and he died at the end of 1808 with the work undone. (See L. V*, n. 1.)]

what we requested his next winter's employment. I do not believe that any thing has yet been done, or is likely to be so, unlefs Mʳ Alderson or some Person, who has influence over him, would go & reside at York & stay with him, till he has compleated his work. For any Person, or any occurrence of the time is sufficient to divert him from it. But unfortunately Mʳ Alderson is now a great sufferer from a most troublesome complaint in his face, the tic doloreux, which confines him principally to his own house: Mʳ Stonhewer is now very weak and infirm from asthma & other complaints, which render him totally unfit for all sorts of businefs, and I have been so great a sufferer from asthma for the last two years as not to < be > able particularly during winter to attend to any thing but my health. I have been travelling about for the last two months in quest of some situation, where I should be able to breathe with ease during the winter months, & after having tried Brighton & the Isle of Wight without succefs, I am now making trial of the climate of Devonshire, which so far suits me better than any other place I have visited before. If I should have a tolerable winter, & should feel myself equal to such a Journey, I shall go into Yorkshire again next summer purposely to make another attempt, & to try if Dʳ Burgh can be prevailed upon to do any thing, or to give up the Papers, which have now been above ten years in his hands. My obligations to Mʳ Mason & my inclinations to do every thing that is right & respectable to his Memory are sufficient motives with me to leave nothing untried, which it may be in my power to do. I am afraid in case of Dʳ B.'s death that the

Papers may get into improper hands and be published in Magazines &c. &c. I have succeeded in carrying one point, viz. not to publish any thing but what M⸣ Mason set his name to, and what he has left in his own handwriting. and this I contend is agreeable not only to the letter but the meaning of his Will, in which M⸣ Stonhewer perfectly agreed with me.—I have troubled you with this letter, supposing that the Bishop of Worcester might not be unwilling to know the reasons why nothing has been yet done respecting M⸣ Mason's works. There was a vile attack on him two or three years ago by D⸣ Miller[4] of Doncaster, published in many of the periodical works. D⸣ M. is a man of very indifferent character, & his indignation against M⸣ Mason was excited by his bestowing his liberality on more worthy objects. I wrote an answer to this scandalous attack, & sent it to M⸣ Alderson for his approbation & correction. He sent it to D⸣ Burgh, from whom he never could recover it either in its original or corrected state. I beg my respectful Comp⸣ˢ to the Bishop of Worcester & remain, Dear Sir,

Your obed⸣ hble Serv⸣

JOHN DIXON

P.S. This letter requires no answer: I shall be satisfied in thinking that it will reach you, & its contents be communicated to the Bishop.

My nephew & M⸣ Mason's Nephew[5] promises to

[4] Edward Miller, Mus.Doc., Author of *History and Antiquities of Doncaster*, 1804.
[5] [William Henry Dixon, son of the Rev. Henry Dixon (brother of John Dixon), who married Mason's half-sister, was

turn out very well. Tho' he will succeed to an estate of 900£ per ann. next Nov.ʳ, He has taken orders, & undertaken the care of a large Parish, & I am glad to hear does his duty in every respect very well.

IV*
RICHARD HURD, Junior, *to*
the Rev. John Dixon
[Extract from a letter]¹

14.ᵗʰ Dec. 1807

As to the Life,² the Bishop says, that after all, the proper Life of a good Poet, or indeed of any good writer, is in his Works. By which he means such as the Author himself has published. For no great account is to be made he thinks of posthumous publications; especially those of genius and imagination.

V*

THE REV. JOHN DIXON *to*
Richard Hurd, junior

London Aug.ᵗ 30.ᵗʰ 1810

My dear Sir.

I was sorry it was not in my power to call upon you at Worcester, when I was at Malvern last November

born in 1783, and after graduating from Pembroke College, Cambridge, was ordained and ultimately became a Canon-Residentiary of York. He collected material for the history of the Cathedral. Mason had left his landed property in trust for him and his brother James.]

¹ [There is a note on the preceding letter "Answ.ᵈ" followed by what is no doubt an extract from Richard Hurd's reply.]

² [Dixon's letter (L. III*) makes no mention of any intention to include a life of Mason in the final edition of his works: but this may have been discussed in other letters that are not extant. (See L. V*, n. 4.)]

twelvemonth. But when my Asthmatic Complaint is troublesome, I am afraid of entering great Towns in winter.

By the death of Dr Burgh[1] & M[r] Stonhewer,[2] the Papers etc. of M[r] Mason have devolved on M[r] Alderson & myself who are both great Invalids. We hope however to print an Edition of his works next spring, with not much new.[3] They are now indeed printing by M[r] Cadell. I have been advised by many of M[r] Mason's Friends to make a collection of his letters in order to enable some competent Person to write his life.[4] I have already made some progreſs—& take the liberty of troubling you with this letter to ask, if there are any letters in your poſseſsion addreſsed to the Bishop of Worcester; & if there are, whether His Lord-

[1] [Dr Burgh died on 26 Dec. 1808 in his 67th year.]
[2] [Richard Stonhewer died on 30 Jan. 1809 aged 81.]
[3] [A note by Richard Hurd states: "A new Edition of M[r] Mason's Works in three volumes with a fourth Volume containing Sermons and an Eſsay not published before was published in 1811 under the care of the Reverend William Alderson son of the Rev. C. Alderson without the intended life of the Author". Mitford, *Walpole-Mason Correspondence*, I, p. xiv, says that the edition was published by John Dixon. Christopher Alderson and Dixon were responsible for the edition, but it may be inferred that owing to their age and infirmities they left the duty of seeing the work through the press to William Alderson, the son of Christopher, who followed him as Rector of Aston.]
[4] [Mason had himself written *Memoirs* of Gray and a *Life* of Whitehead, and it was to be expected that his own life would be written. This may have been regarded as part of Dr Burgh's duty. With the other letters concerning Mason written after his death there is preserved a letter of Sir Edward Littleton (see L. I, n. 10) to Richard Hurd, relating that he had been approached by Mr Dyer, "some time of Emmanuel College", to furnish particulars for a life of Mason. This was George Dyer, the eccentric friend of Lamb. Nothing seems to have come of the project. It appears that as late as 1810 Dixon and Alderson wished to have a life written. Prior, in his *Life of Malone*, p. 307 (quoted by J. W. Draper, *William Mason*, p. 122), says that William Gifford was invited to undertake the work, but he declined.]

ship left any directions respecting them.[5] anything tending to elucidate the Character or Genius of M.ͬ Mason will be of importance. If you will have the goodneſs to favour me with a line on this subject directed to me at Boughton near Northampton, whither I am going in a few days, I shall think myself much obliged to you. I shall remain at Boughton for about a month after I get home & shall then set out for the west of England for the winter, in hopes that I may suffer less from the Asthma than I did last winter.

I was very much amused as well as informed by the Publication of Bishop Warburton's letters.[6]

I remain, Dear Sir,
Your obed.ͭ hble Serv.ͭ
JOHN DIXON

[5] [Bishop Hurd had died on 28 May 1808. His nephew lived at Worcester for some years after his uncle's death and had charge of all his papers (see p. xvi above).]
[6] [*Letters from a late eminent Prelate to one of his Friends* had been prepared for publication by Bishop Hurd in 1795 with directions that the book should be published after his death. It appeared in 1808.]

APPENDIX B

Manuscripts of Poems by Gray and Mason

In the same bundle with the five letters from Hurd to Gray there are copies of Mason's Epitaph on his wife, endorsed by Hurd "Mr Mason's Ep. on his wife in Mr Gray's hand-writing" and of Gray's Epitaph on Mrs Clarke; this is not in the hand of either Gray or Hurd, but Hurd has written at the head of the paper "By Mr Gray".

The text of the epitaph on Mrs Mason does not vary from that printed in Mason's *Works* (I, p. 137). [Mason sent the epitaph to Gray in May 1767, and according to Norton Nicholls, Gray struck out the last four lines, and substituted others of his own. (*Reminiscences of Gray*, by the Rev. Norton Nicholls, see Tovey, II, p. 283.) Gray wrote to Mason on 23 May 1767: "I have shown the Epitaph to no one but Hurd, who entirely approves it. He made no objection but to one line (and that was mine), 'Heav'n lifts', etc., so if you please to make another you may; for my part I rather like it still". (Tovey, III, p. 138.)] The epitaph on Mrs Clarke, the wife of Gray's friend, Dr Clarke, was put up in Beckenham Church. (See Mason, *Poems of Mr Gray*, p. 61.) The copy among Hurd's papers gives presumably an earlier version, and does not contain two lines which are on the mural tablet. On the other side of the paper is written, in the same hand as the English version, an unfinished translation of the epitaph into Latin verse.

168

INDEX

Addison, Joseph, "Virgilian prose", 76; Hurd's edition of his Works, 76 n.; portraits, 98 f.

Aikin, John, on Mason's *English Garden*, 106; on Pope's *Essay on Criticism*, 106

Alderson, Christopher, Mason's executor, xviii n.; Mason's curate, xviii n., 132; Mason's letters to, 95 n.; Stonhewer's letters to, 158 n., 159 n.; Mason's Trustee, 161 n.; Burgh's letters to, 162 n.; responsible for final edition of Mason's works, 166 n.; mentioned, 162, 163, 164, 166

Alderson, William, edited final edition of Mason's works, 166 n.

Aristotle's *Ode to Virtue*, translated by Nevile, 35 f.

Ashby, George, 13 n.

Aston, Mason's Rectory, xvii, 48 n.; Mason rebuilding house, 70; mentioned, 82, 117, 139; Hurd's epitaph on Mason proposed for, 160 n.

Balguy, Thomas, friend of Hurd and Mason, xxii n.; letters of Hurd to, 10 n., 17 n., 80 n.; criticisms of Mason's *Caractacus*, 46; opinion of Rousseau's *Nouvelle Héloïse*, 56; Charge on Subscription to Articles of Religion, 80 n.; mentioned, 23, 36 n., 48, 79, 85

Ball, David, Hurd's curate, 84

Barrington, Shute, Bishop of Durham, 113 n., 129

Bedingfield, Edward, friend of Gray and Mason, 90 ff.

Bellenden, William, *De Statu Libri Tres*, 129 n.

Bickham, James, contemporary of Hurd at Emmanuel, 82 n.

Blaney, Benjamin, Professor of Hebrew at Oxford, 125, 126, 132

Bolingbroke, Viscount, *see* St John, Henry

Boscawen, Hon. Mrs, on Mason's political conversion, 97

Brown, James, President of Pembroke College, Cambridge, and Gray's *Odes*, 36 n., 39

Brown, John, his *Athelstan* and *Barbarossa*, 23 and n.; disliked by Mason, 23 n.; admirer of Gray's *Odes*, 94 n.; mentioned, 11, 38 n.

Brunskill, Michael, Mason's curate, informs Hurd of Mason's death, 157

Burgess, Thomas, Bishop of Salisbury, edition of Horace, *Ad Pisones*, 111 f., 113

Burgh, William, editor of Mason's *English Garden*, 101 n.; delay in preparing final edition of Mason's works, 161 ff., 166

Burke, Edmund, *Vindication of Natural Society*, 28

169

George, Prince of Wales, separation from the Princess, 136 n.

Gibbon, Edward, Hurd's correspondence with, 141 n.; epigram on, 148 n.; mentioned, 142, 148

Gifford, William, invited to write Mason's *Life*, 166 n.

Gilpin, William, friend of Mason, 119

Gisborne, Thomas, M.D., physician, 69 n.

Gisborne, Rev. Thomas, his works, 109 n.; mentioned, 141

Gooch, Sir Thomas, Bishop of Ely, 13 n.

Gower, Lady, 86

Grafton, Duke of, *see* Fitzroy, Augustus Henry

Gray, Thomas, Hurd's letters to, 33, 35, 36, 38, 68; Mason's first acquaintance with, 7 n.; publication of his *Eton Ode*, 7; Hurd's first acquaintance with, 33 n.; Hurd corresponds with, concerning his *edition of Horace*, 33, 35 f.; annotated copy of Milton, 33; gives Hurd his *Odes*, 36; motto on the title page of the *Odes*, 36; Hurd on the reception of his *Odes*, 38 f.; design of writing a history of English Poetry, 37 and n., 68; refusal of the Laureateship, 42 and n.; opinion of Mason's *Elegy on the Death of a Lady*, 49; opinion of Rousseau's *Nouvelle Héloise*, 52; fondness for Crébillon, 52 n.; approval of Hurd's *Dia-*

logues, 64; asked by Hurd to help Thomas Warton, 68 and n.; opinion of Mason's *English Garden*, 69; his *Installation Ode*, 69; Hurd on his character, 78, 104; Mason writing his *Memoirs*, 87, 88 f., 90 ff.; his *De Principiis Cogitandi*, 91 n.; *Ode on Vicissitude* completed by Mason, 91 ff.; mistake in Mason's *Memoirs*, 94; Mason on his character, 106 f.; Mason's epitaph on, not liked by Hurd, 158; urn to his memory at Papplewick, 161 n.; Mason's Epitaph on Mrs Mason in Gray's handwriting at Hartlebury, 168; *Epitaph on Mrs Clarke*, MS. copy at Hartlebury, 168; mentioned, 18, 41, 56

Green, John, Bishop of Lincoln, 79 and nn.

Gregory, George, translator of Lowth's *Praelectiones*, 130, 131

Grey, Zacchary, editor of *Hudibras*, 8

Harcourt, George Simon, Earl of, 96, 150 n.

Hardwicke, Earl of, *see* Yorke, Philip

Hartlebury Castle, xv; Royal visit to, 100 n.

Hayman, Francis, vignette for Mason's *Musæus*, 5

Heberden, William, Hurd's physician, 46 n., 70, 75, 90

Helvetius, *de l'Esprit*, 63 n.

Holdernesse, Earl of, *see* D'Arcy, Robert

171

Mainwaring, 33, 118, 138 n.; chaplain to the King, 39 n.; *Caractacus* read by Pitt, 41 n.; and the Laureateship, 42 and n.; hopes of a canonry at York, 51 n., 55 n., 58; appointed Canon, 158 n.; epigram on Lord Hardwicke and Lord Lyttelton, 54 n.; on Hurd's *Dialogues*, 61; on the plagiarism of Helvetius, 63 n.; Thomas Warton's message to, 64; on Churchill's *Duellist*, 65; rumour of his intended marriage, 65; building a new rectory at Aston, 70; political views, 76 f.; entrusted with Gray's papers, 78; *Elfrida* produced at Covent Garden without his knowledge, 80; talk of settling at Aston, 82; resignation of royal chaplaincy, xxxi n., 83 n.; his Dowagers, Mrs Montagu, Mrs Delany and Lady Gower, 84, 86, 89; Whitsunday Sermon criticised by Hurd, 86; preparing *Memoirs* of Gray, 87 n., 88; quotes Warburton's *bon mot* on Mallet, 89 n.; completes Gray's *Ode on Vicissitude*, 93 n.; inventor of the Celestinette, 93 n.; mistake in *Memoirs of Gray*, 94; interruption of his friendship with Hurd, 95; satirised by Polwhele, 95; political views and activities, 96 f.; change of attitude, 96 f.; loss of Walpole's friendship, 97; resumption of

friendship with Hurd, 97; gives copy of Addison's portrait to Hurd, 98 ff.; persuades Hurd to publish *Life of Warburton*, xxi, 104, 105, 113; on Gray's character, 106 f.; on Hurd's *Life of Warburton*, 110; sends his *Birthday Sonnets* to Hurd, 112, 133, 153; recommends Quassia to Hurd, 115, 117, 123; on *Musical Creeds*, 120 f.; correspondence with Bishop Porteus, 124, 127, 131; on Hebrew Studies, 126, 129, 151 n.; on Mainwaring's *Letter to Lord Sheffield*, 140 f.; present from the Duke of Grafton, 155; death, 156, 157; epitaph on monument in Westminster Abbey, 157 n., 158 f.; epitaph at Aston, 160; urn to his memory at Papplewick, 160 n.; final edition of his works, 161 ff.; attack on, by Dr Miller, 164; proposed life of, 165 f.

WORKS:

Address to Hurd, prefixed to *Ode on Wisdom*, 151 n.
Argentile and Curan, 74
Birth of Fashion, 4 n.
Caractacus, 31 n., 32, 39, 40, 41 n., 43, 44, 48
Elegies, 57 n.
Elegy on the Death of a Lady, 49 n.
Elegy to Hurd, prefixed to *Caractacus*, 44, 46 n.; in *Collected Poems*, 61 n.
Elegy to Miss Pelham, 19 n.
Elegy written in a Church-Yard in South Wales, 98

178

For EU product safety concerns, contact us at Calle de José Abascal, 56–1°,
28003 Madrid, Spain or eugpsr@cambridge.org.

www.ingramcontent.com/pod-product-compliance
Ingram Content Group UK Ltd.
Pitfield, Milton Keynes, MK11 3LW, UK
UKHW012347130625
459647UK00009B/586